LEGENDS OF WAR
THE AIF IN FRANCE
1918

LEGENDS OF WAR
THE AIF IN FRANCE
1918

PAT BEALE

Australian Scholarly

© Pat Beale 2017, 2020

First published 2017 by
Australian Scholarly Publishing Pty Ltd
7 Lt Lothian St Nth, North Melbourne, Vic 3051

Tel: 03 9329 6963 / Fax: 03 9329 5452
enquiry@scholarly.info / www.scholarly.info

ISBN 978-1-925984-63-7

ALL RIGHTS RESERVED

All photos are from the Australian War Memorial Collection.
The cover illustrations are taken from the famous photograph (AWM E02790) of the platoon of Lieutenant Rupert Downes MC, B Company, 29th Battalion. The photograph was taken on 8 August 1918 during the Battle of Amiens, probably at around 8.30 am as the Battalion was about to begin the Second Phase of the battle. Featured are Sergeant Patrick O'Brian, schoolteacher of Gordon, Victoria, aged 24 years, who was killed the following day, and Lewis gunner Private Charles Olive of Lara, Victoria, who was killed on 30 September during the Battle for the Hindenburg Line.

Cover design and cartography: Wayne Saunders

In Memory of
33792 Gunner Octavius Cyril Beale
and for his great grandsons
Dominic, Henry and Daniel

Contents

Acknowledgements .... *ix*
Preface .... *x*
Maps .... *xii*

    1: Legends of War 1
    2: The Defensive Battles – 'Sheep to the Slaughter' – Morale 17
    3: Peaceful Penetration – 'A Pointless Struggle' – Audacity 35
    4: The Battle of Hamel
       – 'Aussies, the Born Soldiers' – Training 49
    5: The Battle of Amiens I
       – 'Fighters, not Soldiers' – Battlecraft 61
    6: The Battle of Amiens II
       – 'Stabbed in the Back' – Tactics/Strategy 81
    7: The Battle of Mont St Quentin
       – 'Lions Led by Donkeys' – Leadership 97
    8: The Hindenburg Line – 'Lovable Larrikin' – Discipline 113
    9: Conclusion 137

Note on Strategy *145*
The Chain of Command in the
Australian Corps and BEF in 1918 .... *147*
Notes *148*
Bibliography *154*
Index *157*
About the Author *161*

Acknowledgements

I am deeply indebted to Professor Claire Woods for her guidance and the time she gave so generously to the proofing and correction of the various drafts. I thank both Colonel Steve Larkins for his encouragement and Professor Peter Stanley for his valuable critical comments and the effort he so kindly gave to the project.

Most particularly I thank my wife Ann Dwyer for her constant support and her cheerful tolerance of the piles of books and papers scattered around the house.

Preface

For many years I have had a deep interest in the First World War (WW1) and, in particular, the achievements of the Australian Corps in France in 1918. I have read widely, attended conferences and given talks but as my knowledge grew so too did nagging concerns. Three issues relating particularly to 1918 kept intruding until I felt compelled to investigate them for my own peace of mind. It is those issues that form the basis of this book.

Firstly, despite so many books relating the course of what happened in 1918 and telling the story of the great battles, there is little analysis of the 'why and how' of the Australian part in the victory. There are many issues to consider. How was it, for example, that the Diggers who had performed stolidly in 1916–17 then evolved into the daring champions of 1918? Why did a force with such a high incident of desertion also have such obviously high morale? From where came the leadership and tactical skills that were so successful? Surprisingly such issues are seldom raised outside the academic conferences of historians or in the works of a handful of experts. I have mined these sources and linked it with my own experience of thirty years as an officer in the Regular Army, a time that included operational service with some intense combat, and the professional study of tactics and strategy. At least I know first hand something of what those men went through and of their skills and capabilities.

Secondly, in seeking answers to the 'why and how', I kept stumbling over legends that have arisen about the war. They are expressed as short shibboleths, convenient 'throw away lines' such as 'lions led by donkeys' and 'lovable larrikin' and each relates to an issue of the 'why and how'. They have however severely distorted our perceptions of the war and our understanding of what happened. From where did these legends come; what was their intent;

and what have been their consequences?

Thirdly, it became apparent to me that as a result of the failure to understand the 'why and how', and the distortions imposed by the legends, we, the Australian public, have arrived at a misperception of the Diggers of 1918. In that last year of the war the Australian Corps won a succession of brilliant victories and the Diggers showed themselves to be among the finest fighting soldiers in the world. Yet there seems a desire to hide their triumph and to remember them as victims. Although it is not how they saw themselves, it is how we now cast them. What happened over the past hundred years that has led us to this distorted impression? It is as if their story has been taken from them, and been rewritten to suit a different agenda. I offer a theory as to what has happened and examine it against the 'why and how'.

Essentially this book is my 'mind clearing exercise' as I sought to answer the questions that had troubled me. Hence it is neither an academic study nor a simple record of events. I provide only a sufficient account of the battles to give context to the issues, and in doing so rely almost exclusively on C.E.W. Bean's Official History. In the analysis of the issues I have turned to the research of a number of the experts such as Dr Ashley Ekins on discipline, Professor John Bourne on the demographics of the command structure and, of course, to Professors Robin Prior's and Trevor Wilson's studies on tactics and strategy. I have also looked at modern theories of such issues as combat stress and leadership and related them back to the period. And finally I have applied my own, first hand, knowledge and experience.

My conclusions will not sit comfortably with everyone. I slap a number of 'sacred cows' on the rump and I challenge some deeply held perceptions. I believe that for too long we have allowed our understanding of 1918 to be clouded by the legends, and for popular authors to compound the misconceptions by dodging the real issues. Not everyone will agree with my conclusions but with that I am happy as long as it induces some thought and discussion. Better open debate than to perpetuate the legends. Hence this book is both a paean to the men of the Australian Corps and to their triumph in 1918, and a plea for a better understanding of how they achieved it.

The Western Front, 1914–18

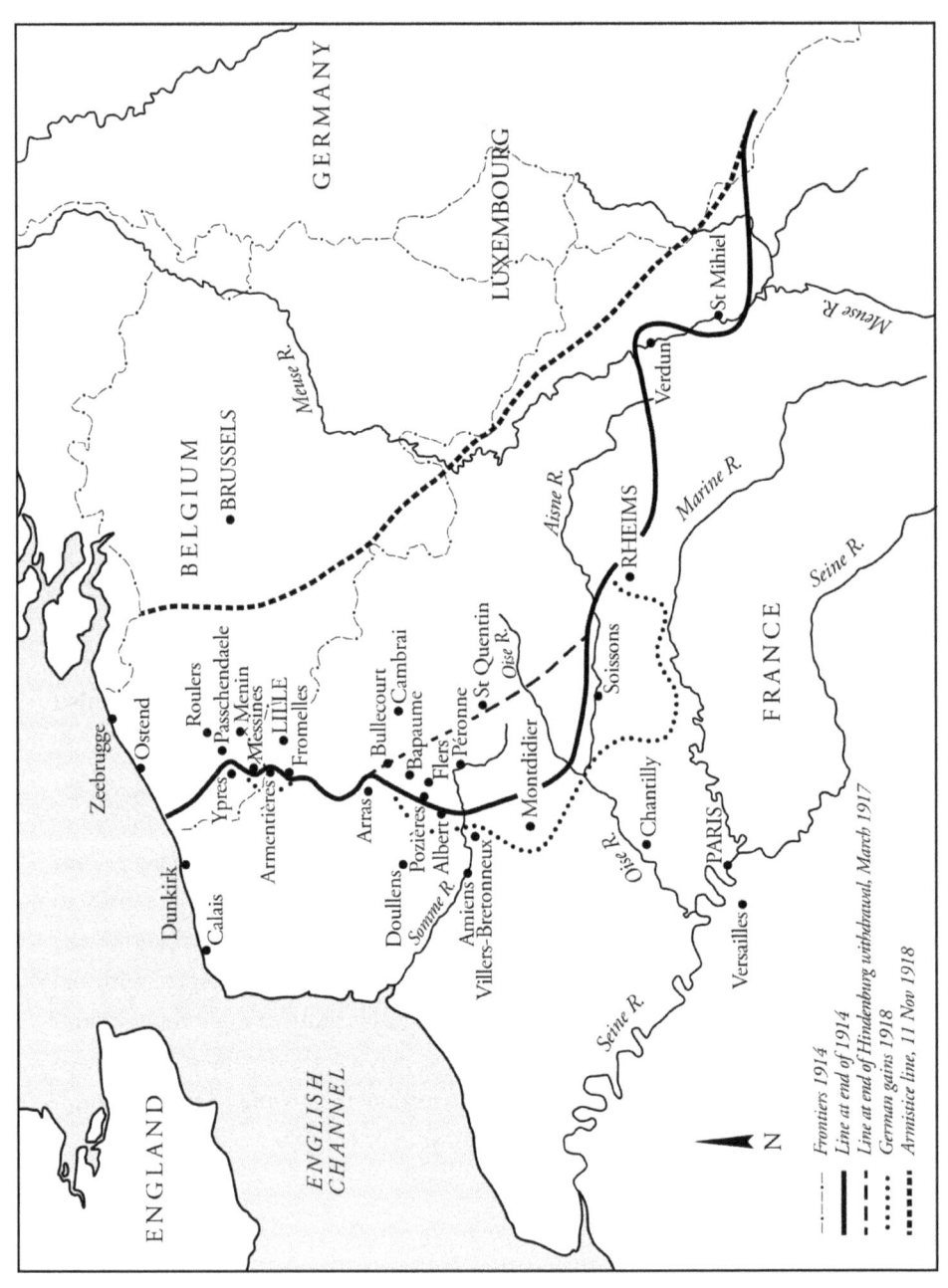

The Advance of the Australian Corps, 4 June – 5 October 1918

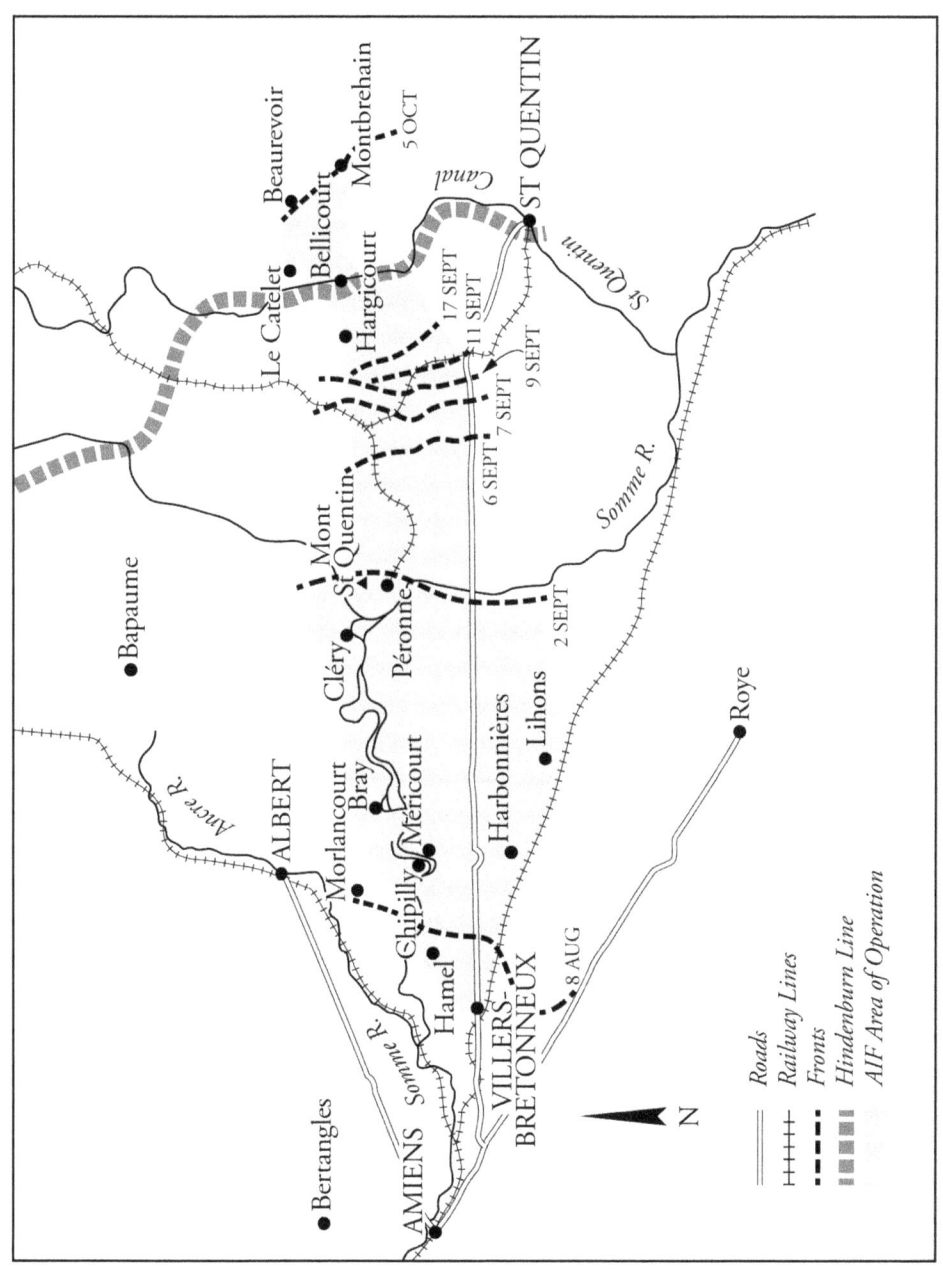

CHAPTER 1

Legends of War

There the screaming and the shouts of triumph rose up together;
Of men killing and men killed and the ground ran blood ...
And far away in the mountains the shepherd hears their thunder;
Such, from the coming together of men, was the shock and the shouting.

The Iliad of Homer[1]

There are essentially two ways of considering Australia's involvement in the First World War (WW1). One is the widely held view of personal sacrifice and futile heroism; of our 'great-hearted men' martyred to a worthless cause, suffering savage losses in a pointless struggle. It is on this perspective we, as a nation, have focused for a century. The other view is of how an initially amateur force, ill disciplined and badly trained, evolved over four years into a highly skilled, well led, and victorious army. Along the way it had suffered stalemate at Gallipoli and then catastrophic losses on the Somme and in Flanders, yet in 1918 rose above the setbacks to play a significant part in the defeat of the German Army and in securing victory. These are two very different perceptions: one negative, the other positive. How can there be such contrasting impressions?

The negative perception of a pointless but heroic struggle has been allowed to become the accepted wisdom. The war is seen to have been a titanic struggle with armies locked in a suicidal embrace; of the soldiers, pawns to incompetent leaders, drowned in a sea of mud, draped on the barbed wire, slapped down by machine guns, or minced by shell-fire. This was a war seen as devoid of any tactical skill; one in which the protagonist stood toe to toe and slugged at each other until one weakened through sheer exhaustion. This is however a very incomplete image of the war. Depending on the depth of the individual's knowledge, this perspective can be seen to be variously as superficial, deceptive or deceitful. To shore up this view of the war requires a scaffolding of legends.

***

Language is constantly changing. The meaning of a word alters with time. Over recent years the words 'story', 'legend' and 'myth' have become entangled in this constant readjustment. 'Simpson and his donkey' was once a story; but is now considered 'a legend', as are also sundry celebrities and sportsmen. The legends that express the public perceptions of WW1 are now popularly referred to as myths. The meanings of the words 'story', 'myth' and 'legend' have become so blurred that to speak with any accuracy it is necessary to turn to the dictionary for their real gist. A myth is 'a traditional story, usually concerning some superhuman being or some alleged person or event and which attempts to explain natural phenomena; especially a traditional story about deities or demigods'. Myths relate to religious or quasi-religious events. We have elevated the story of Gallipoli to that hallowed status and strangely it is assuming an almost sacred aura within our increasingly secular society. Popular usage has seen us erroneously re-titling our legends as myths.

A 'legend' is a 'non-historical or unverifiable story handed down by tradition from earlier times and popularly accepted as historical'.[2] Classicists define legends as traditional stories which, although rooted in historical fact, distort or exaggerate real events. Hence those popular perceptions with which we confuse so much of the reality of WW1 are in fact legends. Legends have always achieved four ends, and do so also in relation to WW1: they provide a simplified explanation for complex events, they mask unpleasant reality, they romanticize questionable behaviour, or they distort reality so it conforms to a different agenda. It is the objective here to look behind these legends of WW1 to recognize their true intent.

***

With great insight a historian of the American Civil War has suggested that 'every war begins as one war and becomes two: that watched by civilians and that fought by soldiers'.[3] Then, as the war ends, the public takes ownership of its memory, often marginalizing the veterans. The *public imagining* of the war may have little relationship to its actuality, therein creating the environment for legends. Few veterans of WW1 would speak about their experience, except among themselves. For the public this left a vacuum that they filled with their imaginings, and from them grew the legends to give substance to those imaginings. In the face of the reticence of the soldiers the public constructed its own perspective of the war. With few exceptions the legends so commonly accepted as reflections of WW1 have civilian origins and present civilian perspectives. Hence it may be illuminating to cast a soldier's eye over the legends and to suggest where the military reality, so important to the Digger, has been disregarded or distorted in the years since, and to seek the reasons why. With the Centenary of the Great War, now is the time to revisit the legends and to seek their origins and the intent behind them.

***

Why should legends play such a major part in our perceptions of the war? In part the answer may lie in the ferment the war created in Australia. WW1 holds a very important, but contradictory, place in Australia's story. Today it is widely seen as a blood-sacrifice, as the integrating event of our national history, unifying a young nation and creating a sombre sense of national identity. Yet at the time, the war was also extraordinarily divisive, splitting those who gave their avid support from those who were stridently opposed. This dichotomy has helped fuel the legends which can be seen either to condemn or to justify both the nation's involvement and the contribution of the Diggers. Some legends are flagrant propaganda; others have been subtly manipulated to give credence to a particular perception. To take the legends at face value is naïve, but to get to their true intent demands close analysis. We should bear in mind that the legends of the war relate to those who fought it – the soldiers – and that fundamentally they are a reflection on those men.

***

Many soldiers coming out of battle are conscious of two conflicting emotions. Firstly, there is the daunting recollection of the personal horror of the experience, and secondly, an elation at the collective triumph of either victory or, at least, survival. The *personal horror* is the consequence of several factors. It is environmental – the noise and violence; and it is psychological – the terror, fear and confusion. The confusion both feeds on and generates fatigue, that in turn saps energy and physical and mental resilience, which leads to debilitating weariness. A tired and confused soldier becomes subject to increased fear which further saps energy.[4] And so the horrible cycle continues. Without some relief, or unless he is uniquely resilient, the soldier will over time spiral into the trauma of combat stress and, in some cases subsequently, into what today is called post-traumatic stress. Any individual coming out of close combat will have experienced this horror to some degree. Its impact will depend on many circumstances, most notably the psychological make-up of the individual, the duration and intensity of the experience, and the perceived support of comrades. However, none will have been immune to the horror.

Contrasting with the personal horror is the conflicting emotion of *collective triumph*. This emotion comes retrospectively, settling in immediately after the experience. It is either the great joy of victory or at least the relief, bordering on elation, at survival, not only of the self but also of the team. Even simply surviving was an achievement worthy of celebration. The triumph is the fierce, almost exultant pride at what has been achieved often at great personal or collective cost. Combat is the most challenging experience an individual can face and survival is usually recognized as having come from a united effort. There is deep bonding with those with whom the experience is shared and who are seen to have contributed to survival leading to a powerful sense of comradeship and team cohesion.

It is difficult for the soldier to express these emotions. To cite the collective triumph seems boastful, and to admit to the personal horror is demeaning. For the Diggers there was also both the 'Edwardian phlegm' and their masculine image to preserve. The breadth, depth and trauma of their experience was too difficult to express: better to try to forget the personal horror, and to save discussion of the collective triumph for the reunions with their mates. The public's lack of understanding of the psyche of the Diggers is savagely portrayed in Alan Seymour's iconic play *The One Day of the Year*.[5] It is bewildering to Hugo why his veteran father should wish to commemorate the day by getting drunk and playing two-up. Hugo fails to recognise that the booze deadens the pain of the personal horror, while the two-up

'The Horror'. Exhausted Diggers rest among the dead and wounded on Broodseinde Ridge during the Battle of Passchendaele, October 1917. Source: AWM E03864

reconstructs the camaraderie of the collective triumph. Alf reflects a century of reticent veterans who have never been able to explain the dichotomy of their experience. In the absence of an explanation the public has foist its perceptions on the veterans and taken ownership of the remembering.

***

When the public took ownership of the memory of the war, some who were more attuned to the psyche of the soldier tried to adapt their imagining to what they conceived to be the personal horror. Yet without experience of combat it was generally too difficult to visualize the environmental and psychological shock of combat. Their only point of certitude lay in the photographic record and that is what has become the basis of the public's perception of the personal horror. There are possibly a dozen iconic photographs of the WW1 battlefield expressive of that horror that would be recognizable to most Australians. What they convey gave an inkling of what the Digger experienced and the public felt it sufficient to claim ownership of what became essentially a very sanitized *public* horror.

The collective triumph was simpler to envisage, at least where a battle was won, although not necessarily where the triumph was only in survival. The difficulty for the public during the war was that they had few relevant benchmarks against which to measure success. It was a totally different war than had ever been fought before. Its weaponry was new – planes, machine-guns, barbed-wire, tanks, and so on. The tactics and techniques that were used were quite alien – creeping barrages, fire and movement, the combined-arms battle, sound-ranging, and strategic bombing. And its character was different from previous conflict. Here the public could find no military glory, no flashing sabres, or waving banners – only the mud and blood and the ghastly casualties. While the public claimed ownership of the collective triumph it did not really understand what that triumph was and their perceptions were easily distorted by the legends.

***

There are now many ways is which the public views the war. It may be visual: through art, movies, documentaries, or its photography. It could be through literature: histories, biographies, novels, plays or poetry. Or via physical contact: through visits to battlefields, memorials or cemeteries. Although the battlefields are far removed we are surrounded by memorabilia of WW1. The war might be fresh and real to us but our perceptions are subject to the distortions imposed by the legends. Unless we can recognize the legends, and know them for what they are, we view WW1 through a glass darkly. Of greatest danger is that the legends can blind us to how the Diggers themselves viewed and reacted to the war. They lived through it, and those who returned continued to live with it for the rest of their lives.

The Diggers' story bears a triple burden of legend. Although the Australian Imperial Force (AIF) was a national entity, it fought as a Dominion contingent of the British Expeditionary Force (BEF). Hence while some legends are uniquely Australian, usually seeking to differentiate the Digger from the Tommy, Australia also shouldered, as befitted its status as a loyal member of the Empire, the British legends of the war. Similarly the British public accepted, and then bequeathed to Australia, those German, French and American legends which suited British public opinion.

Not only do legends hide weaknesses and failure, but they can also obscure achievement. We have allowed negative legends to dominate our perceptions of the war and to shroud what the Australian Corps accomplished in 1918. Why? We need to analyse each legend to establish its origin, motive and consequence. The legends chosen for discussion here are those most often cited in relation to the AIF in France. Each of these legends is commonly expressed by a shibboleth or 'pet phrase'.

***

To give context to the legends they will be examined against the performance of the AIF in the last year of the war in France. The events of 1918 stand out in vivid contrast to those experienced by the Diggers in the first three years of the war. It was almost as if the early years were monochromatic: an endless grey slog of manning the trenches and launching their attacks with varying, but at best, limited success, whether at Gallipoli, in Flanders or on the Somme. 1918 brought a transformation of the battlefield. The German Spring Offensive, which began on 21 March, drove the BEF from the old battle-fields, and it was then fighting in unfamiliar terrain and against new methods, techniques and tactics. Suddenly the divisions of the AIF, which had only recently been consolidated into a single Australian Corps, were called on to apply their bitterly acquired skills in new and very different ways. And they excelled in doing so. Once the German Offensive had been baulked the Allies swung to the attack and, in what is known as the Hundred Days, drove the German Army back until it sued for peace. The Australian Corps played a prominent part in those turbulent six months. Whereas in the previous three years the Diggers had grown to be competent and reliable, in 1918 they were given the opportunity to display their real capability and to demonstrate the skills they had mastered. In just over six months on the Western Front from late March until mid-October 1918, they were engaged in very different forms of war, few of which they had previously experienced. To each they quickly adjusted and gained mastery.

Each of their six major battles of 1918 gives focus to a different legend. Then also the legend can be seen to highlight a particular military competence or virtue. The legends chosen, their popular shibboleths, and their associated virtues are:

'Sheep to the Slaughter'. There remains the belief among many that the soldiers of WW1 were simply cannon-fodder, thrown mercilessly by their leaders into catastrophic battles. This legend is expressed in the shibboleth 'Sheep to the Slaughter'. Why, the public asked, would men face the personal horror of the battlefield? Surely they had to have been driven like sheep. But was this how the Diggers saw themselves? They were volunteers and proud of that status, and by the time they deployed to France in 1916 they were well aware of what they would face. Yet the public persists in accepting a shibboleth that belittles their *morale* and team cohesion. In March and April 1918 the Australian Corps played a significant part in *the defensive battles* that halted the German Spring Offensive. In the face of morale sapping withdrawal, and the loss of the ground gained at such cost over the previous years, the Diggers returned to battle with confidence and even enthusiasm. Why so?

'A Pointless Struggle'. Those who opposed Australia's involvement in the war deride the commitment as a senseless bloodbath. Yet although they condemn it as 'a pointless struggle', that was not how the Diggers saw it. As the Spring Offensive dribbled to an end the Diggers established a moral ascendancy over their enemy through their *audacious* domination of no-mans-land that they termed *Peaceful Penetration*. What accounts for their fighting spirit if what they were doing was so pointless?

'Aussies, the Born Soldiers'. There was a widely held public perception in the young, exuberant nation: that the Digger was 'a skilled bushman, a natural soldier' who needed little, if any, *training*. His natural, inherent skills would triumph on the battlefield. The shibboleth of the 'born soldier' was widely believed, unfortunately, not only by the public but also by the men of the first contingent. Gallipoli brought home brutally the realization of their lack of preparedness for battle. They then set about rectifying the problem. There was an intense focus on training. By early 1918 the Australian Corps was among the best trained forces on the Western Front. The level of skill they had reached was well illustrated by their performance in the cameo Battle of Hamel on 4 July. Yet still the public imagining of the supposed 'natural soldier' persists.

'Stabbed in the Back'. This legend is distinctly different from the others. Towards the end of WW1 the German General Staff fabricated a legend to deflect responsibility for its failure and to lay blame elsewhere for their pending defeat. Their claim, that blame lay with the politicians who had 'stabbed the army in the back', gained wide acceptance and even today still colours the perception among some of the cause of the war's end. The most pernicious consequence of this legend is in its denial of the *tactical skill* of the BEF that led to the great strategic victory of the Battle of Amiens on 8 August in which the Australian Corps played a major part.

'Fighters, not 'Soldiers'. This was a shibboleth thrown by some senior British officers at the Diggers. While reflecting their distaste for Australian dress, drill and discipline it hid a grudging regard for their battle skills. By the time it entered the Battle of Amiens the AIF had perfected its *battlecraft* – the amalgam of individual and team skills needed for success in combat. It was this climactic battle that signalled the start of the Hundred Days, the Allied offensive which culminated in the Armistice on 11 November 1918.

'Lions Led by Donkeys'. This was a universal shibboleth cast against the military leadership of WW1. It reflects a search to 'lay blame' for the horrific casualties of the war. Essentially this legend, and its shibboleth, is an attack on the quality of military *leadership*. Yet there is no better example of Australian leadership, at all levels of command, than in the performance of the Australian Corps at the Battle of Mont St Quentin where it drove the Germans from their intermediate defensive line.

'Lovable Larrikin'. The 'lovable larrikin' is a shibboleth used to disguise concerns relating to *discipline* in the AIF. Initially, just as the AIF was untrained, so too was it ill-disciplined. An army and its individual soldiers depend for their survival on discipline, although not necessarily the rigid discipline of the British army of the day. A unique 'Australian discipline' evolved that was more tolerant than the British. Yet, still embarrassed by the behaviour of the recalcitrants, the public sought to excuse them through this light-hearted shibboleth that masked serious disciplinary issues. These concerns came to a head in the final days of the war. The demands on the Diggers during their victorious assault on the main and final German defences of the Hindenburg Line were extreme. Was discipline collapsing? Was the force disintegrating? Or do we read too much into isolated instances?

The legends have evolved and adjusted over the past century. Many factors have influenced and continue to affect the legends and the ways we interpret them. Before looking at each separate legend in detail we should identify and consider those general factors.

***

It is necessary to look at the legends from their chronological, cultural, social and political perspectives as well as in their military context. Time distorts, taste changes, attitudes alter, and beliefs bend; the legend fashionable today is discredited tomorrow; the political certitude this week may be irrelevant the next; that which is culturally acceptable today may be anathema next year. We must be very cautious of judgements lest we be left looking foolish in time to come. The legends arose from social, political or cultural perspectives of the public imagining of the war. Generally these perspectives reflected the values prevailing at the time. Hence we need to be conscious of the time frame in which each legend arose and the perspective it reflected.

Because the war happened long ago, we tend to see the Diggers as quaint and old fashioned, and hence, condescendingly, to think that they could not be as clever as us today. They, however, confidently knew themselves to be from a society that was at the peak of modernity. They were mostly from cities, and those cities had electricity, running water and, in some instances, even sewerage. There were cars, and trams, gramophones, cameras and moving pictures. They were fighting in an army with the very latest in weapons and equipment. Not for a moment did they consider themselves quaint and old fashioned, nor that their military tactics would be considered wanting, or their leaders be regarded as callous. If judgements must be made, let it be from their perspective. It should be recognised some legends were constructed in later days and reflect attitudes that would have been quite alien to them at the time.

Social values are constantly changing. There is now an emphasis on human or individual rights. Some try to measure the AIF of a hundred years ago against presently popular values despite it being a post-WW2 construct. Too easily we view the period of WW1 with the arrogance of hindsight. When we could still speak to the veterans they were senior citizens, our fathers or grandfathers, and we cloaked them in the wisdom of age. And also, as they were old, we considered them as being a little slow. In the war, however, they had been very young men, the majority between 20 and 24 years of age. Even the leaders were only in early middle-age. They were young men with the confidence, impatience and recklessness of the young. Yet while their behaviour should be familiar, their outlook was markedly different. They were conscious of being from a very young nation and of it being part of the world's greatest empire, and there was great pride in both. They were citizens of a nation-state to which they believed they owed their devotion, and for which they were prepared to sacrifice their comfort, safety and even their lives. These are attitudes almost incomprehensible to us today, but it does them a great disservice to transfer our values onto them and interpret their actions from our present self-obsessed perspectives.

***

Changing political perspectives have impacted heavily on perceptions of the war and hence on the legends. In some regards the legends are all political constructions that reflect the changing popular interpretation of the war. Australia was deeply divided during the war between its supporters and those who were opposed. Some legends can be seen to explain, justify or excuse; others to condemn or belittle involvement. On the one hand, for its duration, those in Britain had stood solidly in support of the morality of the war, although not necessarily in support of the way it was conducted, yet in the next ten years this support changed to condemnation which led to a re-casting of the legends. This phase of re-analysis was then quickly followed by the morale sapping Great Depression of the 1930s, and the tensions arising from German re-armament and resurgent militarism. These circumstances fuelled appeasement and pacifism, leading to re-interpretation of the war and the birth of new legends.

Meanwhile Australian resilience was savaged by the Great Depression and then the Japanese threat of WW2. By 1945 there was recognition that the United States was now the guarantor of our security and then later, as Britain turned to the Common Market, that our economic future lay with Asia. Britain, Europe and with it memory of WW1 became less relevant to Australians. For thirty years, from the 1950s to the 1980s, recollections of the 1st AIF and their great victories of 1918 slowly faded. Those legends arguing the futility of that war then went unchallenged. In Britain, the end of the WW2 and the euphoria of victory quickly gave way to awareness of its new circumstance. The end of Empire, the pervasive fear of a nuclear war and the humiliation of the 1956 Suez Campaign were factors in a time of British social change – in the 1960s its 'Carnaby Street' cultural revolution. Britons sought reasons for their reduced power and influence and looked for 'someone to blame'. WW1 and the Edwardians were convenient whipping-boys to be mocked and old legends were dusted off.

In Australia the sound and fury of the 'anti-Vietnam' and 'Women against Rape' campaigns of the 1970s and early 1980s drowned out even the legends. Recognition of WW1 waned as the zealots did their best to trash the dawn services and any remembrance of war. But when their day passed and their frenzy faded, Australians were left looking for something with which to identify: some event or symbol to represent their nationhood.[6] An effort was made to cast the first settlement in that mould, but Australia Day proved too open to contention, and too Sydney-centric. In 1990 Bob Hawke made the first visit by a prime minister to Gallipoli and the restoration of the myth was underway. The nation then rejected a half-hearted attempt by Paul Keating to construct an alternate myth around Kokoda. Gallipoli was left pre-eminent. Regrettably for some years the focus on Gallipoli obscured the achievements of the AIF on the Western Front. While this has been rectified over recent years the focus has remained fixed on the horror of the battles of 1916 and 1917. There is still a reluctance to remember the magnificence of the part played by the AIF in the eventual triumph over Imperial Germany.

***

Cultural perceptions of the war have heavily influenced the public imagining. Just as social and political attitudes change with time, so too do our perspectives. While during the war popular art and literature tended to accent the 'heroic' and 'the noble-self-sacrifice' this changed markedly over the following ten years[7]. The traditionalist canvases of Septimus Power of guns being galloped into action, George Lambert's square-jawed portraits and Arthur Streeton's poignant landscapes that offered only glimpses of the carnage, were supplanted in public popularity by Will Longstreet's ethereal *Menin Gate at Midnight* which caught the immediate post-war grief. This was followed quickly by the stark and brutal chaos of the modernists' depiction of the battlefield, imagery that reflected the public imagining of the 1920s and 30s that was abetted by the stark battlefield photography of Frank Hurley and Hubert Wilkins. The focus of the art had swung from the triumphalism of the traditionalist to the personal horror of the modernists.

It is noteworthy that there was little published Australian war-related fiction or biography in the years shortly following the war. While in Britain in the late 1920s there was a surge of biographies, some thinly veiled as fiction, and poetry by young veterans, there was only one of note by an Australian, Frederick Manning's *Her Privates We*, yet even this was based on his service with a British battalion. The influence of these predominantly British writers, notably Siegfried Sassoon, Robert Graves and Edmund Blunden, and the poet Wilfred Owen, on the Australian public imagining was deep and abiding, and re-enforced the personal horror.[8]

The Australian contribution to the war literature has been primarily in historical accounts. General Sir John Monash led the charge with his *Australian Victories in France in 1918,* published within six months of the end of the war, and was then followed by a spate of battalion histories. C.E.W. (Charles) Bean set the standard with his 12-volume Official History, of which he personally authored six volumes. Australia has been subsequently gifted with eminent military historians such as Robin Pryor and Trevor Wilson, whose research has cast a spotlight on the Western Front and set the benchmark for the present generation of academic military historians. It is sad however that their diligent research has failed to capture the attention of the public or alter the public imagining. The Centenary now sees a flood of books for the populist market, updating Bean with modern vernacular. Many capitalize on the horror with a focus on Gallipoli and the catastrophic battles of 1916 and 17. The writers often show little understanding of war and their efforts largely obscure the reality and re-enforce the legends.

Much of the more recent focus of the writing in Australia of WW1 has been on the personal records of the Diggers through their diaries and letters. Bill Gammage led the surge for this genre with his book *The Broken Years*. While this approach gives an intimate and immediate quality to the story it runs the risks, that often the Digger was concealing or distorting, either deliberately or unintentionally, much of the reality of his experience. This was often to shield his loved-ones from the horror, but could also be his reluctance to boast of his triumphs. While a few revelled in recounting tales of the blood and gore, most were too inarticulate or considerate to burden their families with the reality.

***

The nation's 'architecture-of-memory' reflects the imagining.[9] The memorials are a constant reminder to the community of the war. Even after a hundred years they have a pervasive influence on the imagining that seems to be growing rather than fading. The stolid magnificence of the Australian War Memorial, the capital city cenotaphs, the memorials in little country towns and in the suburbs, even simple honour boards in sporting clubs, school halls and council chambers, are a constant reminder. They are many and varied: plain obelisks, statuary, crosses of sacrifice, memorial gardens and walls, avenues of trees, public halls and water troughs. Their simplicity or extravagance signifies only the relative affluence of that particular community, rather its commitment to remembrance. Often a simple honour board can convey poignancy as powerfully as a stately marble cenotaph. The accent, though, is invariably on the grief and personal horror.

The iconography is almost exclusively sombre; reflective angels with folded wings, soldiers 'resting on their arms reversed', downcast gaze, stolid architecture. Here was no place for glorifying monuments, arcs of triumph, soaring columns, or heroic statuary. The public's imagining of the war demanded a solemn and sedate imagery: reflective of the horror, the pain and the suffering. The memorials were not seen as the place to record their victories or their triumphs. The state capital memorials are generally stately tombs in the form of mausoleums. Even at the Australian War Memorial, their story is discretely tucked away beneath the cenotaph. Why were the Diggers denied the recognition of their triumph?

The memorials played an important role in the lives of the families who had lost members. Those killed were interred on the other side of the world. The cost of travel precluded most families from ever visiting the grave. Hence the local memorials assumed a twin role of a place of reflection and also of grieving. They became the surrogate grave-sites for bereaved families. For most of the century commemoration on the iconic Anzac and Remembrance Days has taken the form of a funeral service rather than one of reflection. They have acquired a special vocabulary, often redolent with such phrases as 'noble sacrifice', 'martyrdom', and 'giving up his life for others' which, while comforting, is seldom true. The dawn services reflect the public imagining of the personal horror. Any suggestion of the collective triumph on these occasions is construed as 'glorifying war'.

***

If we are to get something approaching a clear perspective of the Diggers and the AIF we need to look beyond the legends and try to un-clutter our minds of long-established prejudices. War is always shrouded in legend but WW1 is obscured by heavy fog. That fog descended most densely over the final year of the war and the part played in it by the BEF and its Dominion contingents in achieving victory.

The Diggers who deployed to France in mid-1916 were smarting still from what they perceived as their failure in the Gallipoli campaign. Through 1916 and 1917 the five divisions of the AIF fought the meat-grinder battles of the Somme and Flanders, learning cruelly that it took more than dash and raw courage to overcome a well-entrenched enemy protected by barbed wire, machine guns and artillery defensive fire. They, with the rest of the BEF, were on a steady learning curve, at the cost of hundreds of thousands of casualties, to learn how to defeat their skilled enemy. However, by the time the AIF came out of Passchendaele in October 1917 they had started to acquire the tactics and techniques to match the Germans.

1918 was a year of triumph for the AIF but sadly the public imagining, informed by the legends, has denied them the recognition of their great achievement. From late March to early October, they displayed the military qualities of sound leadership and training, high morale and audacity, skill in battlecraft and tactics, and mature discipline. They applied these qualities in several phases of war that showed their adaptability and flexibility. They achieved great things but, as always in WW1, at heavy cost. Their casualties of around 50,000 in 1918 were as cruel as that suffered the previous year in the wretched battles of Bullecourt, Messines and Passchendaele. The public was unable to differentiate between the losses sustained in the earlier heroic but futile battles and those suffered in the course of achieving victory. Our perspective of the war has been distorted by the legends. It is time to scrutinise them, to seek their origins, their intent, and to recognise their consequences.

CHAPTER 2

The Defensive Battles

'Sheep to the slaughter'

Morale

What passing bells for those who die as cattle?
Only the monstrous anger of the guns.
Only the stuttering rifles' rapid rattle
Can patter out their hasty orisons.
No mockeries for them from prayers or bells,
Nor any voice of mourning save the choirs, –
The shrill, demented choirs of wailing shells;
And bugles calling for them from sad shires.

Wilfred Owen[10]

The shibboleth of 'sheep to the slaughter' is probably of post-Napoleonic French origin with the 'sheep' being the often heavily bearded French soldiers, or *poilu,* 'the hairy ones' of the Second Republic, a nickname that remained popular in WW1, when the French soldier was still allowed to grow a beard. To the French public it was a descriptive of affection. Then in a display of gallows humor the *poilu* went bleating into battle in the disastrous Chemin des Dames offensive of 1917. It was the losses in that battle which led to widespread mutinies[11] within the French Army. The shibboleth was then transferred to the Tommy in the Flanders battles of Third Ypres of late 1917, battles fought at great cost, in part to distract German attention from the wounded French Army. In its transfer to English lexicon the shibboleth took on a belittling and condemnatory tone: the sheep were dull and witless.

The soldier, who believes that he is 'herded' into battle and that his leaders see his life as of no more worth than that of a sheep, will understandably have low morale, and yet to an army morale is of crucial importance. Poor morale becomes most apparent in a crisis. While the sun shines all may appear fine and an army can delude itself. When the clouds gather the need for morale will become apparent. For the BEF its worst crisis of the war came with the German Spring Offensive in March 1918. Within weeks it had lost the ground gained at enormous cost over the previous three years. Its casualties rivalled those of the bloody Passchendaele losses of the previous year. Even its commander-in-chief, Field Marshal Sir Douglas Haig, conceded British backs were to the wall. The fate of the BEF now depended on its morale. The previous year had seen the collapse of the Russian army, the French 'troubles', and nearly the rout of the Italians at Caporetto. But in 1918 the BEF held on by the skin of its teeth. The Australian divisions were hastily brought back from reserve or quiet sectors to help meet the crisis. What was the impact of the Spring Offensive on the morale of the Australian Corps? Did the Digger see himself herded sheep-like back into battle?

***

The German offensive was launched on 21 March. Since the Russian surrender late the previous year the German Chief of Staff, General Eric Ludendorff, had been shifting troops back from the Eastern Front. With 35 extra divisions German strength at last exceeded the allies: 190 German divisions opposed

A German assault. Source: AWM H12331

175. An attack was inevitable and it had to be soon: before the influx of American divisions tipped the scales irrevocably against Germany. Although the offensive was anticipated, where it would fall was not known and it came as a surprise when the first phase, Operation Michael, struck primarily the British Fifth Army, holding the longest and most lightly defended sector of the British line.[12] At the southern flank of the BEF it both shielded the strategically vital city of Amiens and linked the British and French armies.

Not only did the blow fall in an unexpected sector but it employed new tactics and techniques that came as a surprise. The battle opened before dawn with an unprecedented barrage from 6,400 guns. Over the next five hours the barrage, rich with gas shells, swept from the front trenches to the depth defences and gun-lines and then forward again, saturating the objectives. Then the Storm divisions, the elite of the German infantry, were unleashed with the task of swift penetration, by-passing resistance which was left to be mopped-up by the following, lesser skilled and equipped, Trench divisions.

***

The British Fifth Army, holding 68 kilometres of front with twelve under-strength divisions, bore the brunt of the German push. They were attacked by 43 German divisions. As could be expected, by the end of the first day, the BEF had lost 250 square kilometres, 21,000 prisoners and 500 guns. Over the next two weeks it was pushed back across the battlefields of the Somme where in the past years so much blood had been shed in taking each square metre. But remarkably the Fifth Army was not destroyed: its survivors fought a ragged but dogged withdrawal and prevented a German breakthrough. The name of the commander of the Fifth Army still resonates negatively with many Australians. General Sir Hubert Gough had Australian divisions under his command when they fought their most bloody, and seemingly futile, battles at Pozieres, Bullecourt and Passchendaele. He is associated in many Australian minds with senseless slaughter. Yet in the face of Operation Michael he had his finest hour.

From a brigadier-general commanding a cavalry brigade in 1914, in less than two years he had risen rapidly, through the patronage of Haig, to the command of an army. Contrary to popular perceptions he was more often in the front line than any of his fellow generals: his courage can never be in dispute. It was possibly a family attribute as his father, brother and uncle were all VC recipients. He was, however, noted for three other traits. He showed a reluctance to delegate, reflecting a lack of trust, which led to his taking, and hence being accountable for, decisions that should have been the responsibility of his subordinates or staff. He was impetuous and acted often on impulse. Thirdly, he was stubborn. It seems that once set on a course he would try to push it to its conclusion regardless of the consequences, and the consequences were often the lives of his soldiers.

It was probably his aggressiveness that appealed to Haig and which, together with his relative youth, made him stand out. Born in 1870, he was much younger than the other army commanders and he was even five years younger than Monash. Those his age were more likely to be commanding divisions in 1918. Ironically it was in withdrawal rather than attack that Gough finally proved his worth. It was largely to his credit that the British were able to make a fighting withdrawal, keeping the line intact and denying the Germans a breakthrough. But by April Gough was gone, sacked; the scapegoat demanded by the politicians.

This is not an apologia for Gough: but to give some context to a subset of an Australian legend. It is now belatedly recognized that it was his aggressiveness and stubbornness, those very characteristics for which we condemn him, that very likely saved the front from being broken open and possibly the war lost. His greatest contribution to allied victory was in saving it from defeat. The Fifth Army was disbanded and replaced by a resurrected Fourth Army under the command of General Sir Henry Rawlinson, who was shortly to have the Australian Corps under his command for the remainder of the war.

By the time the offensive began the five Australian divisions had at last been united into a single Australian Corps.[13] They remained under the command of the seconded British officer, Lieutenant-General Sir William Birdwood, and were resting in the north from their exertions at Passchendaele, either in reserve or in the quiet trenches near Messines. As Operation Michael erupted the divisions were successively dispatched south to help block the German threat to Amiens and by 5 April all bar the 1st Division had been relocated.

***

By 25 March the situation seemed so dire that Marshal Henri-Philippe Petain, the French commander, seeing his left flank exposed, and worried that it posed a threat to Paris, threatened to draw back his armies, which would have left the BEF isolated and facing piecemeal defeat. Although the offensive had failed to achieve a breakthrough it had still resulted in schism within the alliance. In consequence came the appointment of a supreme commander, a position that fell appropriately to the pugnacious and determined Marshal Ferdinand Foch. This at last brought long-needed co-ordination of the allied efforts.[14]

By early April Ludendorff could see that Operation Michael had failed to achieve a break-through and that it was losing momentum, consequently he planned to unleash the second phase of the offensive Operation Georgette. Georgette was to be launched in the north on a 32-kilometre front by 12 divisions with the objective of Hazebrouck and the Channel ports. Hazebrouck in the north mirrored Amiens in the south as a vital logistics centre and nodal point for rail communications on which the flow of supply to the BEF depended. And while Amiens was a gateway to Paris, the loss of Hazebrouck would open the Channel ports to the Germans with the threat of isolating the BEF from Britain. When the new phase of the offensive began on 9 April the storm-troopers quickly routed the Portuguese divisions holding Fromelles and in the next few days over-ran the old Flanders battlefields. Again the BEF was in withdrawal, but the situation was judged more critical than it had been in the south, leading Haig on 11 April to issue an uncharacteristically emotional appeal to British morale: 'Every position must be held to the last man: there must be no retirement. With our backs to the wall, and believing in the justice of our cause, each one of us must fight on to the end.'[15]

The 1st Division, the last to be sent south to join the rest of the Corps near Amiens, was hurriedly recalled and deployed in front of Hazebrouck. Australian divisions were now holding the approaches to the vital ground at both the north and south of the British line. Haig must have had confidence in Australian morale.

***

The Australians, marching south, were warmly welcomed as potential saviours by the French villagers, who were either fleeing with what belongings they could manage or waiting fatalistically for whatever would eventuate. All records suggest the Diggers arrived confident and enthusiastic, and eager to get back to grips with the Germans. By 1918 they were seasoned soldiers who knew both what was expected of them and also how to do it. They had been toughened by their experience over the previous three years, which had bred resilience in the individual and confidence in the team.

On 28 March the 4th Division was the first into action with Sergeant Stan McDougall winning the Victoria Cross for blocking a German attack on the village of Dernancourt north of Amiens[16]. He then, several days later, was also awarded a Military Medal, repelling another, an even more determined attack on the same village. Meanwhile Brigadier-General Charles Rosenthal's 9th Brigade had moved further south to positions behind Villers-Bretonneux. Rosenthal had recently taken command of the brigade. He had a robust and forceful personality and a love of challenge. He thrived on combat and was frequently at the front as his many wounds attested.

Now at Villers-Bretonneux began the long and close relationship between that French town and the AIF. Sixteen kilometres from Amiens, it was crucial to the defence of the city. From nearby highpoints and from just west of the town it was possible to look down over the lip of the Santerre plateau into Amiens, and critically into its railyards and logistics dumps. Villers-Bretonneux was vital ground; holding it was critical.

The German advance threatened the town but an assault by the 33rd Battalion, led by Lieutenant Colonel Leslie Morshead, pushed the Germans back a kilometre to the east. Morshead, who had risen in rank from lieutenant at Gallipoli, was described by Bean as 'a dapper little schoolteacher, only 28 years of age'[17] but with a high reputation that would be further enhanced in his command of Tobruk in WW2. The attack was well planned and competently executed and the town was secured but the Germans, recognising its importance, continued their build up over the next few days. On 4 April the Germans attacked and Rosenthal's 9th Brigade fought the first battle for Villers-Bretonneux: a rolling scrum of precipitous withdrawals and violent counter-attacks that left the town in Australian hands at the end of the day. Villers-Bretonneux had been saved but at the cost 665 Australian casualties. The day had been finally won by an assault by the 36th Battalion across much the same ground as traversed by the 33rd Battalion on 28 March. In the course of the attack one young officer, Lieutenant Albert Amess, who had been blown off his feet by a shell that morning, was hit by a sniper through the arm. He carried on. When all the other officers in his company had become casualties he took over but was hit again by a sniper. He carried on. Later, leading a rush he took another bullet through the shoulder. He carried on. That evening, while directing the consolidation of the company defences, he was hit once more and finally was half-carried by his batman to battalion headquarters for 'a long and close examination as to the situation' before finally being released for treatment.

On that day the 9th Brigade had several factors in its favour. Despite its march from the north it was relatively fresh and with good numbers while its opponents were exhausted and depleted by two weeks of constant combat. The Germans, however, had momentum, confidence and the high morale bred by success. Yet the Diggers held them and turned them back. Their morale proved superior. Operation Michael had reached its high-water mark. It had cost the allies nearly a quarter of a million casualties and the total loss of 2500 square kilometres of territory, but the German momentum had ebbed away and their focus now swung to Operation Georgette.

***

It was Napoleon who stated words to the effect that 'morale is to the physical as four is to one', and military history is replete with tales of small determined forces triumphing over larger, less motivated, opponents. High morale, that sense of well-being and confidence which is so important to soldiers, can be very fickle. It can arise quickly and from unlikely events, from even something as trivial as removing a heavy pack at the end of a long day's march. It can be ephemeral and dissolve on reading a bad letter from home, yet conversely may survive a bloody set-back. The image we have of the Somme battlefield, and of the personal horror faced by the men who fought, leaves us wondering how there was any prospect of high morale. Yet the Diggers' morale was solid and, as the months of 1918 passed, it appeared to grow even stronger. Morale is not conferred from on high, neither does it come up with the rations. Yet without high morale ability to fight effectively is reduced. Morale helps the soldier to contain his fear in battle, helps him rise above the personal horror and to fight to the best of his ability. And with high morale his zeal will inspire his comrades. There are two closely linked terms; morale, which relates to the individual, and esprit de corps, which is its collective equivalent.

Esprit de corps is the spirit of pride in the team; pride that ultimately determines the effectiveness of that team. A unit with high esprit functions as a unified team. A team with confidence in itself and in its leaders will be prepared to take the risks that win battles. In many ways the two, morale and esprit, are inseparable. A unit with esprit will bolster morale in its members. Men with high morale will inspire esprit in the unit. High morale and esprit are battle-winners: they help contain the personal horror and re-enforce the collective triumph.

Just as a leader cannot impose morale neither can esprit be ordered into existence. Yet while the fighting spirit of his force should be the primary concern of its commander all he can offer to create that esprit is to provide a foundation of leadership, discipline, training and tradition on which esprit can grow. What then accounts for the high morale of the Diggers in 1918?

As long as men have fought together in armies a primary inspiration has been the example set by their predecessors. Tradition has always played an important role in the esprit of armies. The stories of the past – the traditions and the legends – set the example to the soldier and inspires his fighting spirit. The traditions take many forms; distinctive forms of dress, embellishments to uniforms, styles of drill, regimental colours, and special days honouring past victories. They exist to give the sense of belonging and to provide a foundation for esprit.

This panoply was something denied the Diggers. The histories of their battalions extended over only four years at most. They had no regimental colours emblazoned with past battle-honours, no traditions, rituals or customs to which to cling. They did not even have their own distinctive battalion badges; all simply wore the 'rising sun' badge of the AIF. Their only distinguishing mark was their unit flash – a piece of cloth of particular shape and colour, distinctive to each unit, which was sown on the shoulder of their jackets. In the place of regimental colours were only home-made tattered banners on which were usually painted the battalion's number and its colour patch. Yet this lack of the panoply of war seemed to have little impact on their esprit. These men seemed to take a particular pride in their institutional poverty and looked instead to creating their own traditions.

There is a strong co-relation between esprit and discipline. While discipline has connotations of mindless obedience and rigid conformity, there is its other perspective of a group working in unity to a common purpose. Without discipline a military force cannot function: yet without esprit it cannot function effectively. As will be seen later, the Diggers had issues with discipline and it took time to establish a uniquely Australian style of discipline that suited the individualistic Australian volunteer but, when achieved, it buttressed their morale. Once it became a disciplined force then morale flourished. The strain of the last six months of 1918 with its constant battle challenged the discipline of the Australian Corps but its esprit helped contain the problem. Morale and discipline are complementary and both inter-relate with leadership.

There can be no doubt that part of the high morale of the Australian Corps was the product of the leadership style that had evolved in the AIF. While this will be considered later in greater detail, it must be recognized as a major contributor to their morale. That he had confidence in his leaders, at each successive tier of command, was crucially important to the Digger's morale, particularly if he was to put his life in jeopardy on the orders of those leaders. The soldier would respond positively to leaders he knew and respected and in whose judgement he had confidence. That confidence extended upwards from the corporal who yelled 'charge', to the general who said 'take that hill'. The Digger knew his corporal and platoon commander well. They were likely men who had joined the battalion at the same time, with whom he had fought previous battles, and were possibly old friends with whom he had grown up from boyhood. Equivalently, he had seen the senior officers, the battalion, brigade and division commanders, rise through the ranks over the preceding years and he knew that now the best were at the top.

The battles of Villers-Bretonneux were notable for the active part played by three of the most renowned fight-leaders of the AIF, the Brigadier-Generals Rosenthal, Glasgow and Elliott. They were forceful men and each with his own strong style of leadership: Glasgow of quiet determination, Rosenthal by personal example and Elliott with flair and bombast. They were universally admired throughout the AIF and Rosenthal and Glasgow were shortly to be given command of divisions while Elliott knew he should have been. The Digger's confidence in his leaders assumed a major place in his high morale.

Just as morale stems from discipline and leadership so too is it reliant on the soldier's confidence in the quality of his training, his battlecraft and in the tactics he employs. His morale requires a belief that in battle he will both survive and win. He will fight against great odds if he believes he will be victorious. So too will his morale be enhanced with confidence in the superiority of his weapons over those of his enemy. By the time the battalions of the Australian Corps came marching south to confront Operation Michael they were highly trained and had confidence in their equipment and their skill as soldiers. Many factors then can be seen to impact on morale and all are issues that are considered in greater detail in subsequent chapters. It becomes important to recognize the interaction and inter-relationship between tradition, discipline, leadership, training and morale. There remains, however, a final determinate of morale – that of the quality of the soldier himself.

***

Ultimately morale depends on the ability of the individual to manage his fears. We tend to regard morale as something bestowed on the individual but seldom do we consider it as self-generated. We recognize morale as a reflection of the soldier's confidence in his mates, his team, and his leaders, but seldom as a product of his own self-confidence in his skill and his ability to adapt to his environment. While for the Digger that environment was horrendous, in most instances, with the support of his mates, he rose above its horror, leaving him more or less in charge of himself. Most achieved that level of self-control and it is reflected in their determined attitude with which they faced the trauma of combat. By 1918 they were tough, seasoned soldiers, all volunteers, and with a growing reputation of which they were proud.

The morale of the Digger was also dependent on his friends and comrades. While mateship, the bond of close friendship, is in no way uniquely Australian, we as a nation try to claim it to ourselves. There are those who theorize that our focus on mateship derives from colonial times. The isolated shepherd and stockman are seen to have been very dependent on the companionship of their other few lonely comrades. Yet despite few Diggers coming from rural backgrounds, the horrors of the WW1 battlefield led men into mutual dependence. A sympathetic ear with which to share the fears was crucial to many to maintain control in the face of the personal horror. So too was the team with whom the Digger lived and fought important to his morale.

***

It should be recognized that there were significant differences in the structure of the AIF from that of the British Army. First and foremost, by 1918 most British soldiers were conscripts, and the removal of the element of choice from his service impacted on his morale. Secondly, the British military system emphasized the county-based regiment where its soldiers were allocated to any of the many battalions of the regiment. The Australian system was of State oriented battalions, each quite separate and distinct entities and not linked in regiments. The Digger's loyalty was to his battalion while the Tommy's was to the far larger and less personalised regiment. In Australia friends, brothers, members of the local cricket or football team enlisted in the same battalion, and brought with them established bonds of friendship.

Separated from home and country for the duration of the war, the battalion became the surrogate 'home' of the Digger. Unlike the Tommy he could not return to his true home on leave several times a year. While the Digger had frequent leave it was in impersonal cities in which he was a stranger. He lacked access to family or civilian friends. This made the Digger dependent on the close bond with his comrades and it was a mutual dependence, resulting from their isolation from home. The bonding with his 'army family' became very important and was carried forward post war into the strong battalion and veteran associations.

Although by 1918 battle had taken its terrible toll and few of the originals remained, their successors had absorbed the old ethos and carried forward the same battalion spirit. It was common that up to seven times the original numbers passed through a battalion over the course of the war, yet if anything the bonding of the men grew tighter. To its members the battalion became home, providing security, comfort and comradeship. The bond with the battalion is no more clearly shown than when, towards the end of the Hundred Days, the AIF came its closest to mutiny. Some under-strength battalions were to be broken up and their members distributed as re-enforcements to other battalions. In every instance there was flat refusal to amalgamate, and in some cases the men continued to fight as battalion entities under their own elected leaders after their officers and senior NCOs had departed. This issue of discipline is examined in greater detail later. It is a sad footnote to the battles of Villers-Bretonneux that the first batch of disbandment fell on those brigades that had fought the two battles. The 36th Battalion, which had performed so valiantly on 4 April, together with the 47th and 52nd, were all disbanded by the end of April.

***

Throughout the war the Australian public hung upon news from the front and there was wide public pride in the achievement of its soldiers. Yet by the early 1930s, as the post-war years passed, attitudes had changed. There had been a significant switch in the public's perception of the Digger. Their imagining had swung from admiration to one of pity of men they now regarded as having been 'led like sheep to the slaughter'. What accounts for this transformation in the image of the Digger in the minds of the public? Why should the quintessential hero of 1918 be regarded as a 'the sacrificial lamb' by the 1930s? Possibly the public was trying to empathize with the personal horror rather than remembering the collective triumph. Then possibly other more immediately contemporary issues were already starting to cloud recollections of the past. Several factors were in play.

After the frenetic 1920s dark clouds gathered. Totalitarian states were emerging: Stalin, Hitler and Mussolini had taken power. The hapless League of Nations was irresolute in the face of the Italian invasion of Ethiopia and the Japanese grab of Manchuria. Political instability followed the economic chaos of the Wall Street crash of 1929 and the subsequent Great Depression. The hopes and dreams of world order and stability that had marked the war's end had been ephemeral. The sacrifice of so many lives was now regarded as having been for naught. While the British intent of 1914 had been simply to halt German aggression, as the war progressed a new objective arose, a utopian dream of 'the war to end all wars', and in that context it was now seen to have been a palpable failure. Hence, although its original purpose had been met, the failure to attain world harmony now condemned the enterprise. In consequence those who had fought were considered to have been duped and to have been sent like sheep to the slaughter. This 1930s culture of pessimism was then fed by complementary factors.

While in Australia during the war there had been many who were strongly opposed to the war, in Britain there was almost universal support for the principles for which it was fought, despite criticism of the way it was conducted. Yet in Britain this had been turned around within ten years and there was wide and vocal condemnation of the war. A number of British historians have now remarked on this shift in popular opinion in the 1930s. It is thought to have been in part the consequence of the prevailing political and economic instability but also of the failure at the end of the war to have given the public a clear explanation of the contribution to victory by the BEF. The animosity of Prime Minister David Lloyd George towards the military leadership left him loathe to credit them with victory. This deprived the people of their collective triumph and led them to dwell on the personal horror. It was then compounded in the following years.

Books, in the absence of TV and Twitter, remained the most powerful medium to shape public opinion. In the 1920s there was a wave of biographies of the wartime leaders, both the generals and the politicians were intent on justifying their actions. They revealed to the public the tensions that had existed between the British Government and its Army leadership. Known as 'the battle of the bios', the bickering that was revealed set the scene for disillusion. This was followed in the early 1930s by a surge of books by the young men who had done the fighting. Historians over the past fifteen years conclude that the writings of the British veterans had a profound, and unintended, impact on the people's perception of the war. These books, including among many others, those of Robert Graves, Edmund Blunden, Seigfried Sassoon, the Australian, Frederick Manning (writing of his experiences with a British battalion), and the poems of Wilfred Owen were as avidly received in Australia as in Britain. The authors were primarily young, English public school men with little experience of hardship and previously, none of war. They had been junior officers and their perspective of war was from the trenches. While their theme was seldom pacifism, and few dwelt exclusively on the personal horror, such was how the public tended to interpret them[18].

Lacking any balancing story of collective triumph, the focus swung to the public horror. This British re-interpretation was widely accepted in Australia. That the writing by young British officers related to British soldiers, and reflected values and attitudes that were different to those of the volunteer Digger, was disregarded. By the 1930s the Australian public seemed unable to differentiate between the Digger and the Tommy: it seemed the popular perception was that 'if it was good enough for the Tommy to be a 'sacrificial lamb' then it was good enough for the volunteer Digger'.

***

Throughout April the struggle for ownership of Villers-Bretonneux continued.[19] The Germans were intent on retaking the town which they signalled with heavy gas attacks on 16 and 17 April that inflicted 650 casualties on the Australians. The defence of the town then passed to the British 8th Division which, after heavy losses from Operation Michael, had been re-enforced with drafts of very young conscripts who observers likened to school-children. The Germans shelled the town from 4.45 on 24 April and then followed with an assault supported by tanks. This was too much for the inexperienced conscripts: the town fell, together with 2000 prisoners. Half-hearted counter-attacks during the day failed.

By 1918 the difference between the Tommy and the Digger was stark. After its massive expansion in early 1916 the AIF had consolidated over the following two years into a tightly bonded and cohesive force. Their unity grew as their numbers declined through casualties and waning recruiting. What was left was a rump of increasingly tired but highly skilled soldiers. In contrast the British Army was in its third stage of flux. The professional elite of the 'Old Contemptables' had fallen at Mons and Ypres in 1914; the volunteers of 'Kitchener's Army' at Ypres II in 1915, and their conscript successors in the battles of the Somme in 1916 and Ypres III of 1917. Britain was dipping ever deeper into its pool of manpower. By April 1918 the threat of Operation Michael was demanding that 17- and 18-year olds, with only a couple of weeks training, be dispatched to the front. It is unkind to compare these youngsters to the battle-hardened Diggers. For them there had been little chance to build team cohesion or to acquire the skills of the seasoned AIF. That they performed as well as they did is to the credit of British junior leadership, where at last there was promotion based on experience as well as breeding. The British Army was increasingly reliant on the survivors in its ranks to step forward with their skills as the junior leaders.

***

In recognition of its importance to the defence of Amiens, the re-capture of Villers-Bretonneux was demanded by Rawlinson, Haig and Foch. Consequently, on the next day, 25 April, the Australian 13th Brigade was sent marching south where, together with the 15th Brigade already located just north of the town, both were put under the operational control of the British 8th Division. The commander of the 13th Brigade, Brigadier General William Glasgow, reported to Major General William Heneker, commander of the 8th Division, and found confusion. Successive higher levels of command, through corps to army, were interfering in the planning, giving Heneker conflicting orders for the counter-attack. Glasgow assessed the situation, made his own plan, including the direction and timing. He insisted it be a night attack by the two Australian brigades. The 15th Brigade had been sitting north of Villers-Bretonneux for some days, and its commander, Brigadier General Harold (Pompey) Elliott, had already arrived at his own counter-attack plan that generally aligned with Glasgow's concept. The main difference was Glasgow's determination that the attack be by night. Both plans were for the town to be enveloped: the 15th Brigade attacking to the east across the open ground north of the town, while the 13th Brigade would strike parallel on the southern flank. The two brigades would meet east of the town at a prominent feature, the Monument. Poor Heneker, trying to comply with the wishes of his superiors, must have been nonplussed when the two Australian brigadiers, the dour but emphatic Glasgow and the excitable and domineering Elliott, effectively took control out of his hands and imposed their own plan.

As well as being a night attack there was other great complexity to the operation. While the 15th Brigade had ample time to view its sector and plan in detail, the 13th Brigade could not arrive until after dark, following a long march, then shake out and attack over ground with which it was totally unfamiliar. To compound the problem, Heneker was not sure of the location of all British troops following the German attack, and believed the woods on the right of the axis of the 13th Brigade was still in British hands. Neither could the attack be covered by a barrage as the guns were not registered. Glasgow had his battalion commanders collected from the marching columns and driven to Heneker's headquarters, where he briefed them and sent them back to their battalions to issue their orders on the march. Meanwhile Glasgow drove to Elliott's headquarters to co-ordinate the action of the two brigades and then established his own command post close to Elliott's.

Showing extraordinary skill the 13th Brigade, having sent ahead its intelligence staff to locate and mark the forming-up place and the start-line, arrived, deployed and attacked as planned at 10 pm. The men were far from fresh, having been marching since 11 that morning. Their assault soon came under heavy machine-gun fire from the woods to their right, supposedly occupied by the British. Casualties were heavy until a platoon, on its own initiative, detached itself from the assault and cleared it in savage hand-to-hand combat.

The 13th Brigade continued its assault; an attack in the dark to a depth of nearly half a kilometre, over ground it had never seen, that contained thick wire obstacles and with the enemy occupying both flanks. The attack was drenched with German machine-gun fire, even after the woods on the right flank were cleared. The only illumination was from burning buildings in Villers-Bretonneux and German flares which silhouetted the attackers for the machine-guns. It was a hard, dogged battle, but they advanced, clearing out the German trenches, negotiating the large barbed-wire obstacle that stretched diagonally across their front and fending off the counter-attacks launched at them. Much of it was heavy hand-to-hand combat. It was costly and heroic but the brigade slogged its way forward, eventually stopping just short of the Monument.

Meanwhile the 15th Brigade on the northern flank fought a different battle. For days it had overlooked the ground and had planned for this assault should it be needed. While their start was delayed, the going was easier and initially it faced less opposition. Then, half way to the objective, there was a strange development. The Diggers began to yell and cheer and shortly they seemed to be grasped by a collective hysteria and they went rampaging forward, virtually out of control. They fought like berserkers giving no quarter, sparing no German who tried to surrender. Bean records 'the men had thrown off the restraints of civilized intercourse and … [had become] primitive, savage men'. The assault swept beyond its objective before the leaders were able, with difficulty, to re-establish control and get them back to the objective. Bean cites only two comparable events with such behaviour: the Landing at Gallipoli (three years earlier to the day) and at the forthcoming Battle of Mont St Quentin.

When they stopped and consolidated the two brigades had nearly met and the gap was covered by observation and machine-gun fire which meant Villers-Bretonneux was effectively encircled. The following morning the two brigades linked and the town was cleared. The two Australian brigades had counter-attacked two elite German divisions and had won decisively; the 13th Brigade had over-run the 4th Guards Division and the 15th Brigade shattered the 228th Division. The conventional formula of a ratio of 3:1 in favour of the attacker had been inverted. It was a heroic achievement. It had, however, been at a heavy cost: the 15th Brigade suffered 455 casualties while the 13th Brigade lost 1009. Over 50% of those of the 13th Brigade who had crossed the start-line had become casualties but the rest had pressed on.

***

The victory of the two brigades on Anzac Day 1918 was one of Australia's greatest feats of arms that gained wide recognition at the time. In many ways it established the status of the Australian Corps as an elite force. Henceforth it was marked by Rawlinson and Haig for important tasks. It set the scene for its further exploits through the year to its culmination at the Hindenburg Line six months later. It would be a hard six months, fighting all the way, but they had established their reputation and dominance. They had shown again that they were tough and adaptable soldiers: and once more that they could be wild and savage fighters. To have tackled this challenge in the way they did showed men with very high morale, and units with great esprit de corps. Only a donkey would mistake these lions for sheep – or else it is someone with malicious intent to denigrate or trivialise their achievement.

***

By the end of April both German offensives, Operations Michael and Georgette, had failed. While the initial barrage and the scheme of infiltration had succeeded, the storm-troopers had failed in the intent of breaking through and managed only in forcing the defenders, admittedly at great cost, backwards. Worse, the Germans had now to defend unfamiliar ground where they had no established defences. Then too they had forced the BEF back close to its logistics centres, while they were now separated, at the end of a lengthened line of communication, from their own supplies. In consequence the German defences for the next four months were rudimentary, and this was to play a part in the next set of battles. In turn this new German vulnerability encouraged Australian morale which led to a new and audacious approach to battle.

CHAPTER 3

Peaceful Penetration

'A Pointless Struggle'

Audacity

The derangement of war was all around me: dust that dimmed the sunlight, the noise of crashing chariots and splintering wood, elephants and horses calling, bones and metal breaking, and shouts and cries of warriors.

Mahabharata[20]

There were those who condemned Australia's involvement in WW1. They considered it as a pointless struggle in which Australia should not have been involved. This opposition came from two elements in the community. There were the clamorous socialists opposed on ideological grounds and also elements of the large Australian-Irish community who held strong anti-British bias and did not believe it was Australia's war to fight.[21] Those of Irish descent, comprising about one third of the population in 1914, were predominantly Catholic and saw themselves as partly excluded from mainstream Australian society by the Anglo-Protestant majority. Their opposition to the war was not shared by all those of Irish descent. The number of Australian-Irish who served was proportional to their percentage of the general population, and from them came many of the great figures of the AIF, but there remained a rump of vocal opposition.

Their argument reflected their resentment of their social exclusion, and their opposition was fired by the Irish Rebellion of Easter 1916, by the referendums on conscription, and by the rallying figure of the Irish Archbishop of Melbourne, Daniel Mannix, but it went wider and deeper than those alone. To the Australian-Irish nationalists it was a pointless struggle because it was a British imperialist war, concerned only with British power, in which Australia should not be involved. Some still, to the third generation, cling to this belief and remain dismissive of the sacrifice and the triumph, despite the part played by many of their fellow Australian-Irish.

The other faction, the socialists, included many, but by no means all, of the governing Labor Party, whose leader Billy Hughes championed the war. The Party split over conscription and in 1916 Hughes and twenty-four members were expelled. Undaunted, he eventually formed a coalition Nationalist Party and retained the Prime-ministership. Many of the socialists saw the war in ideological terms as a struggle for supremacy between competing European capitalist states. To them the war was a capitalist conflict that in its course would exploit and oppress the workers and it must therefore be opposed. They condemned it as senseless slaughter and some to this day still continue to belittle Australia's involvement in the war and those who fought in it.

***

This left Australia as a divided society with both strong support and virulent opposition to the war.[22] Both camps sought to legitimise their causes with 'foundation myths'. The Left had been constructing their myth around the bushman and the shearers' strike of the 1890s.[23] Then, from 1915, they were challenged by the creation of a rival myth. Public attention focused on Gallipoli. The myth that was created suits a conveniently classical mould of a founding war. It contains great heroism and sacrifice, a courageous and honourable opponent, a measurable battlefield and a precise start and finish. There was a hero figure in Simpson and his donkey and even a villain – the British – to blame. It has all the ingredients for a plausible foundation myth. And it has become established as the de facto national day, which is ironic as it was a failure, but also a blessing in that such a disastrous campaign could never support a glorification of war. Its very failure induces solemnity, self-examination and sombre contemplation of our future. Sadly, however, its popular acceptance has detracted from recognition of the achievements of the AIF on the Western Front. That was a struggle too complex and too bloody for public glorification. Meanwhile the socialists found their shearers' strike had been trumped, and even their anthem of *Waltzing Matilda* had been stolen as the Diggers' song. They later sought alternatives in a hypothetical '1942 Battle of Australia' or, with greater legitimacy, the Kokoda campaign. Neither, though, has grasped the public imagination and Gallipoli has become firmly entrenched as the acknowledged popular choice.

***

Few would dispute that all war is intrinsically a 'pointless struggle' yet the nature of society and our political structure is such that we are fated to war. Some would have found it ironic that Australian-Irish nationalists and socialists would have condemned the violence of this particular war yet otherwise have condoned violence in support of their respective causes. The war began for a multitude of reasons, a cauldron of ambitions, fears, jealousies, petty dynastic rivalries, long-standing disputes, the death of an archduke, and even the vagaries of railway timetables. Britain's engagement was on a different plane where, as the guarantor of Belgium's neutrality, its involvement became a moral obligation when Germany violated that neutrality. The Diggers would have seen that Australia's status as a loyal dominion made inevitable its support of Britain, regardless of Australian-Irish sentiment and socialist ideology.

A recruiting march that left Wagga Wagga in December 1915 with 86 men and after 350 miles arrived in Sydney with 230. Source: AWM H11586

Recent studies also reveal a German intent for a 'greater Germany' that made an eventual continental war inevitable. While in 1914 the Kaiser may have preferred the war began later, it was still going to occur. And, if Britain became involved in that war, then so too would Australia. Should Britain have been defeated then Australia as a British dominion, regardless of whether it was engaged or not in the conflict, would have been occupied, subjugated and forced to pay reparations which, if German demands on Russia in 1918 at the Treaty of Brest Litovsk are indicative, would have been crippling.[24] By 1914 Australia was becoming part of the world order and its involvement was inescapable, but some failed or refused to realize it.

***

The upshot of the divided society, the prolonged war, and the focus on the horror, was a critical fall-off in recruiting. By 1918 the euphoric days of late 1914 were long gone. The patriotic enthusiasm to fight for 'king and country' or to 'teach the Hun a lesson' had ebbed away with the casualty lists from Gallipoli. In its place there came a sense of civic duty, of obligation to be with mates or brothers already fighting, of not being seen to be a shirker and, undoubtedly among some, the unarticulated 'right of passage' of the young man setting out to meet this challenge to his manhood. A few, ignoring the odds, still joined to escape the law, the wife, or for the pay. But the numbers were dwindling rapidly. From early 1918 there was a looming manpower crisis in the AIF. Yet the Diggers fought on, and with increasing skill and vigour. Their morale was at its peak. Why should this be so in view of the dangers they faced?

***

Their numbers were declining because of the horrific casualties they were sustaining. In their two and a half years in France and Flanders they suffered the equivalent of around 57 killed each day which, to give it context, is more per day than were lost in total in the ADF's recent ten-year engagement in Afghanistan. Yet theirs was a stoic acceptance of the odds. Most would have shared the sense of 'the immortality of youth', the conviction that he, the individual, would survive regardless of what may happen to his mates. As the war continued its seemingly endless course, each must have considered his probable fate. There came a fatalistic acceptance of the odds, but always the conviction that 'copping-it' would be delayed and come 'in the next push, not this one'. That most faced it with such equanimity demonstrates their strong morale. It also reflects their mental toughness and resilience and a very different attitude to death.

We seem now to believe that only the elderly are allowed to die. In the event of younger deaths it is accompanied by counselling and grief management for the bereaved, an outpouring of public anguish and often an ostentatious display of lamentation. In the community of 1918 it was regarded much more pragmatically, and on the battlefield the Digger was surrounded by death. He lived with corpses and the stench of death. He witnessed death daily and few had not lost comrades and good friends. No soldiers have ever confronted death more constantly. Bean casually records a patrol of the 32nd Battalion, to be led by a Lieutenant Cecil Treasure,[25] on the night of 18th April on which a shell fell short as they gathered to depart, killing one and wounding two, whereon the patrol was deferred. Bean then recounts that: 'On the following night, however, going out with a dozen men, he met a German patrol of twenty. With his revolver Treasure shot its leader. His Lewis gunner quickly killed six more, and the patrol returned with a prisoner.' There was an acceptance of violence and death that is now, after only one hundred years, very much at odds with present attitudes.

To understand the Digger and to relate to his attitudes requires an empathy with his values. The most difficult we face is in recognizing his acceptance of the reality and proximity of death. He had a robustness in the face of adversity that society now lacks. All the same, it did not shield him from the long-term consequences of his experience which came back to haunt him or his mates after the war. Post-traumatic stress has been only recently classified, and then untitled it took a terrible toll on the returned soldiers.

***

As Operations Michael and Georgette dribbled away to inconclusive ends a new phase of operations began. As well as leaving the Germans at the end of an extended line of communications, a consequence of the offensive had been to force the BEF back onto a fresh battlefield. No longer was the war waged in the pitted moonscape of the 1917 Somme and Flanders battlefields, but now it was fought in largely rural terrain often little scarred by war. While in places it lay on partly recovered 1916 battlefields or in open rolling country, much of it now offered cover and concealment with ditches, sunken roads, hedgerows, copses, and ruins of small villages not yet obliterated. The spring crops planted before the German offensive were growing strongly and offered further cover from view.

The Diggers adapted quickly and seized the new environment as their own. Through their raids, active patrolling, sniping and small-scale attacks they soon established their dominance. They termed their activities 'Peaceful Penetration'[26] as a play on the pre-war description of German trading methods of infiltrating British overseas markets and taking them over by stealth. This new phase of Peaceful Penetration would last for three months, only a tenth of the time of the AIF in France, but it left a lasting legacy. Its long-term impact on Australian Army doctrine was established. Its continuing emphasis on patrolling, to 'dominate the battlefield', can be traced back through WW2 to Peaceful Penetration. The need to own 'the two-way range where the targets shoot back', or 'the-ground-beyond-the-wire', was imbedded in the psyche of the Australian infantry from 1918. It accounts for its success (and sometimes survival) from Tobruk and Tarakan to Tarin Kowt.

***

Through April there was a struggle for control of no-mans-land. The Germans still had the impetus derived from the tactical success of their offensive, while the Australians had their newly won confidence. Initially there was a succession of patrol clashes and little battles with the honours shared, until steadily the Diggers gained ascendancy. By the end of April the Australians owned no-mans-land and from then on the Corps was seldom challenged. Nor was Peaceful Penetration the only tribulation faced by the Germans. Interrogation of prisoners and captured letters and documents showed that artillery harassing fire, the sudden shelling of a frequented spot at random times, was a constant drain on German numbers and morale, as too was the unexpected strafing by aircraft.[27]

The Germans were steadily losing their aura of invincibility in the eyes of the Diggers: 'the savage Hun' was morphing into 'poor old Fritz'. The confidence of the Digger in his superiority over his enemy was rapidly growing. With that confidence came a new quality. The Australian soldier had never lacked courage as had been shown time and again in such struggles as the Neck, Lone Pine, Pozieres and Passchendaele. He would fight with great determination, bravery and self-sacrifice, but now a new factor was emerging, that special attribute of a supremely confident soldier: audacity. Throughout the Corps, from the soldiers to the generals, there was a bold self-confidence that encouraged them to take the gamble, to seize the opportunity, to 'give it a go'. It is such acts of daring, often made spontaneously, that can win battles. And the confidence to take the initiative was established in the Corps by the success of Peaceful Penetration.

Bravery, courage, heroism and even valour are positive responses but they are essentially a reaction to a situation. A quick and aggressive response can swing the situation back in one's favour; but it remains a response to an existing situation. Audacity however is unique in that it is the making of the situation in the first place. It is a calculated act of boldness: seeing and seizing an opportunity. For the soldier it is accompanied by a heightened level of risk, yet survival figures prominently in both a soldier's thoughts and his reactions. Audacity demands he must go beyond normal considerations of self-preservation to new heights of boldness. What was remarkable was that in mid-1918 this audacious behaviour was often originating directly from the soldiers themselves. The Diggers were not simply responding to threats but were initiating them spontaneously. What accounts for this quite dramatic change in their behaviour? Bean records that at this time there was 'a buoyancy and initiative beyond all expectation to the perpetual wonder of their own officers … Undoubtedly it arose from their perception that now, at last, their efforts were visibly counting towards the stopping of the Germans, the protection of the French people, and the winning of the war'.[28] This may well have been so but whether the Digger thought in such lofty terms is debatable. Probably their new-found audacity stemmed as much from two other factors.

They had been living and fighting together now for three years. Within each battalion there was great team cohesion; the men knew each other well, including their strengths and weaknesses, and they respected each other and also sought the recognition and approval of their comrades. Some were prepared to take actions to prove their worth and to cement their place in the team by acts of daring. And they were prepared to take the risks because of their confidence of the support of the other members of the team.

The other factor was the mutual trust that now existed between the men and their leaders. The junior officers, the platoon and company commanders, were men who had risen from the same ranks as those they now led, and they were admired and their peccadilloes were known and tolerated. And now at this time there was the 'Australianisation' of the higher command. Nearly all the senior appointments were in Australian hands as the best brigadier-generals stepped up to take over the divisions and they were succeeded by the best of the battalion commanders. The men knew and approved and there was a strong sense of unity within the Corps. The new commanders knew their men well and were prepared to give them their head. The Rosenthals, Elliotts, Glasgows *et al* had confidence in their men and, recognizing that confidence, the men reciprocated with ever more daring behaviour.

***

The Germans' defensive tactics played into the Australian's hands. The second-grade Trench divisions were under-strength, less well trained, motivated or equipped, and were left longer in the line without relief or rest. Further, German tactics, while successful against major attacks, were a liability when challenged by Peaceful Penetration. The main defences were sited up to two kilometres behind the forward defended localities, which were lightly held as section posts, with even more isolated sentries and listening posts deployed to their front. Spread so thinly, the forward troops were left not only lonely and nervous, but they lacked the man-power to develop their trenches or to build meaningful wire obstacles, further enhancing their vulnerability.[29] They offered an irresistible target to the confident Diggers.

Initially there was a fear that the Germans were preparing to renew their offensive against the BEF and this gave impetus to identifying which German formations they were facing, particularly whether or not Shock divisions were in the vicinity. This demanded the capture of prisoners, identity discs and documents. At this the Diggers became adept. Bean several times refers to the instance of Sergeant John Bruggy[30] of the 3rd Battalion, outside Hazebrouck, who one day dropped six German ID disks on his company commander's table. His explanation of how he had acquired them was not believed so he led the Company Sergeant Major out, crawling 400 metres through a corn crop to a German emplacement containing two dead and two mortally wounded Germans and the marks of where a further two badly wounded had crawled away, all of whom Bruggy had shot on his one-man raid. Such individual enterprise was not unique.

***

The third phase of the German Spring Offensive began on 27 May but it fell on the French Army in the Champagne district west of Rhiems. It followed the established German pattern and the French were quickly driven back to the River Marne. Although this presented one of the most serious crises of the war the effect upon the Australians was to allow a change of focus from gathering intelligence to the deepening of their front. Rosenthal's 9th Brigade had moved from Villers-Bretonneux to the open rolling hills in front of Morlancourt to the north of Amiens. Here there was no chance of a covert approach to the German lines so a different technique was employed. On moonless nights they simply advanced their positions, overrunning the very thin German screen and occupying their ground. It was achieved with minimal casualties and led to their steadily taking more and more terrain and eventually occupying the critical high ground.[31] And always with Rosenthal playing an active role at the front.

The constant night harassment to which they were subject kept the German troops awake at night. In consequence the warm summer days made sleep inviting. Lieutenant Arthur Irvine, the Intelligence Officer of the 18th Battalion, in the Morlancourt area, noting a heavy silence from the German lines late one morning, called for volunteers and, lining the eighteen men out at two-metre intervals, led them quickly and quietly across to the German trench and returned shortly, without casualties or a shot being fired, and with twenty-two prisoners, including an officer and a light machine-gun.[32]

The success of the Battle of Hamel on 5 July, in which the line was advanced by one and a half kilometres on a frontage of six kilometres, led to plans for a repeat of the battle to deepen the line in front of Villers-Bretonneux. Yet before the plans could be finalized the objective had been secured by 'nibbling' to the depth of one kilometre on a four-kilometre frontage, at a cost of a quarter of the casualties suffered at Hamel. Over a period of two weeks the ground was taken by a succession of small-scale actions: here a patrol taking a German post, there a quick company night attack seizing a hundred metres of trench. All the time nudging the line further forward. It was the accumulated results of a series of small, bold actions by leaders from corporal to colonel. Some were carefully planned battalion operations while others were spontaneous initiatives by a handful of Diggers. It was achieved by two brigades of the 2nd Division, now commanded by the newly promoted Major General Rosenthal. Inspecting the front on 19 July Rosenthal was wounded, this time seriously, by a German sniper.[33]

***

One of the most widely recounted acts of audacity is that of Staff-Sergeant Jack Hayes[34] and his small band of comrades on 9 August, the second day of the Battle of Amiens. The Australian success on the previous day had not been matched by III Corps, their flanking formation on the north bank of the Somme. There a ridge, the Chipilly spur, projected into the Australian flank and from it came constant German machine-gun and mortar fire that was an irritant to the 1st Battalion on the south bank. Over two days the 2/10th London Battalion had failed to clear the spur. On the evening of 9 August Hayes, a company quarter-master sergeant of the 1st Battalion, with his friend Sergeant Harold Andrews and four soldiers were told to cross the river, find out what was delaying the attack and help where possible.

At 6 pm they crossed the river, found the company of the 2/10 London, rejected the advice not to proceed and, shaking out, attacked and cleared the village of Chipilly and brought up the British. An attack in which Hayes was to lead a British platoon was then frustrated by an unexpected barrage of British smoke shells. It, however, gave cover for the Australians to approach another German machine-gun post but in the process of rushing it they stumbled across a further position which they also took. Continuing, they came across dugouts from which 32 Germans surrendered. These were passed to the Londoners following behind. Two of Hayes's soldiers then captured nine men and two machine-guns. Finally a further 30 surrendered to the same pair. Having cleared the Germans from the spur in three hours, a task a hundred Londoners had been unable to achieve in two days, the six Australians returned at 10 pm across the Somme.

***

One of Bean's great achievements was in personalising his history of the war. So often in military history we read in detail of the behaviour of the leader but the soldier often remains a cipher. Bean takes the story to the Diggers and we read of the achievements of individuals and of the valour of the 'common soldier'. It does carry the risk that from this point in time, a hundred years after the events, we may trivialise the accounts by viewing them from a 'Boys Own' perspective of 'dashing tales of derring-do'. We should recognise these were the actions of real men, not fictional characters. It took raw courage and sheer guts for those men to again and again defy the odds of their survival and take the risks they did. When we talk of audacity we should recognize that it was achieved by will-power overcoming the natural impulse for survival. It may appear in print to have been a game, but in reality it was deadly serious: a matter truly of life or death. Yet above all we should recognize that usually these acts of valour were the product of personal choice and initiative. Often these men were putting their lives at risk, not because they had been ordered or led to that point, but because they chose to do so. It is likely that Peaceful Penetration was a phenomenon rather unique in the history of warfare.

***

Bean recounts many dozens of examples of the success of Peaceful Penetration. Here we shall conclude with one further example of the boldness now common among the Diggers. On 28 June the British division on the flank of the 1st Division at Hazebrouck was to launch a limited attack, which the 1st Division was to support by simulating an attack by noise and with a barrage. The commanding officer of the 10th Battalion, Lieutenant Colonel Maurice Wilder-Neligan, saw the possibility of using the demonstration to the battalion's advantage and warned his subordinates to be alert for any opportunity.[35] Seizing such a chance was typical of Neligan, a notably competent and aggressive officer who had risen from being a company clerk at Gallipoli to the command of his battalion. It was an invitation readily accepted by Sergeant Tom Leathley who, around 6 am, taking advantage of the close vegetation of the area, led a party of four men against a German post, capturing three and killing two.

Hearing of this success his company commander sent forward a platoon which took another 20 prisoners. Meanwhile another platoon commander with one man had taken another five prisoners in an adjoining field. Neligan, seeing the opportunity, now intervened, and at 8 am had the two forward companies advance to where the German posts had been over-run. For the rest of the morning there was close and confused fighting. Neligan, recognizing that the German posts were now in very close proximity to his new line, decided to push them back and, after a successful barrage, launched his reserve company in an attack at 6pm. By the end of the day the battalion had captured 500 metres of the German front and had taken 35 prisoners and 6 machine-guns but at the cost of about 50 casualties. The success was noted by the new commander of the 1st Division, Major General Glasgow.

***

There was recognition of the audacity of the Australian Corps. General Sir Herbert Plumer, highly regarded by the Diggers, in whose Second Army the 1st Division had been operating, farewelled them with the comment 'that there is no division, certainly in my army, perhaps the whole British Army, which has done more to destroy the morale of the enemy than the 1st Australian Division'[36]. Even German regimental historians concede the impact of Peaceful Penetration. One, writing also of the 1st Division, records that: 'justice demands recognition of the fact that the enemy here was an unusually daring and enterprising soldiery which often pressed our front line heavily and grabbed many posts from us', while another records: 'the enemy here opposed to the division was … an exceptionally daring, tough and enterprising soldiery'.[37]

***

This phase of Peaceful Penetration was of great importance to the Australian Corps. It allowed a period of consolidation. Leaders of proven competence moved to their new appointments. Monash took command of the Corps; Glasgow, Rosenthal and Gellibrand rose to command divisions, while the proven Sinclair-MacLagan, and Hobbs, remained in place. All were now Australian with the exception of Sinclair-MacLagan who, while British Army, had been serving with the Australians since before the war when he had been on the staff of the Royal Military College. Bright young men moved up to succeed them in the brigades. They were all of proven quality and their promotion was applauded. A new generation of leaders was established with the physical and mental robustness that would be needed for the heavy demands of the Hundred Days.

The static nature of the phase gave the Diggers the chance to draw breath, and to recover their strength. It was the time to train and to trial new techniques, and to accept the few new recruits available and to absorb them into the battalions. Above all the phase gave them new confidence. Through Peaceful Penetration they proved their status as outstanding soldiers. These men knew this was no futile struggle. They had the measure of their enemy and they knew it. The public, however, was oblivious to what the Diggers were achieving. Peaceful Penetration was hardly news-worthy so their audacity went largely un-remarked.

***

As time passes and we draw further away from the 20th century and view its course holistically it is possible to detect a continuum in the wars of the century. It is now suggested that WW1 was the first round of an epochal conflict in which parliamentary democracy withstood the totalitarian challenge of proto-fascism (WW1), fascism (WW2), and communism (the Cold War). This epochal conflict, extending from 1914 to 1990, has been dubbed the Long War.[38] If viewed in this context the significance of WW1 is altered and it rises above considerations of dynastic squabbles, economic rivalry, or grabs for land and power. It is a complex concept that is beyond the scope of this book but which would cast both the sacrifice of life and the shibboleth of a 'pointless struggle' in new and very different perspectives. It may be that future generations, removed through time from the horror of the slaughter, will come to see the war as having played a special part in the march of democracy. Far from being a 'pointless struggle' the suffering and loss of life may be seen to have been a sacrifice by that generation for the preservation of our chosen way of life.

CHAPTER 4

The Battle of Hamel

'Aussies, the Born Soldiers'

Training

Today we have naming of parts. Yesterday,
We had daily cleaning. And tomorrow morning,
We shall have what to do after firing. But today,
Today we have naming of parts. Japonica
Glistens like coral in all the neighbouring gardens,
And today we have naming of parts.

And this you can see is the bolt. The purpose of this
Is to open the breech as you see. We can slide it
Rapidly backwards and forwards: we call this
Easing the spring. And rapidly backwards and forwards
The early bees are assaulting and fumbling the flowers:
They call it easing the spring.

Henry Reed[39]

In 1914 few Australians had knowledge of the nature of war, much less of the complexity of modern war that would be unleashed over the next four years. Few recognized that to fight effectively an army and its soldiers must be exhaustively trained for the task. There was a naïve belief that 'the bronzed Anzac was a natural soldier' who needed no training. This view stemmed from the over-weaning self-assuredness of the vibrant young nation. There was a strong sense of achievement that bred illusions, and among these was the belief that, in having tamed the continent and its challenging bush, then, ergo, all Australians were in a sense bushmen. And as bushmen they were 'natural soldiers and crack shots'. It was an illusion that dangerously masked shortcomings in the AIF, notably the lack of their soldiers' real skills and training.

The idea that they were natural soldiers was embraced by those enlisting in 1914. They were keen to be seen as Australian soldiers and not be lumped in with the Tommies. Although the term 'Digger' did not evolve until 1917 they sought early to differentiate themselves as either 'Aussies' or, after Gallipoli, as 'Anzacs'. They believed they had an innate superiority as 'natural soldiers' and it was a view encouraged by journalistic hyperbole. The renowned British war-correspondent, Ellis Ashmead-Bartlett, despite not arriving at Anzac Cove until 15 hours after the landing, was able to report that 'the Australians rose to the occasion. They did not wait for orders, or for the boats to reach the beach, but sprung into the sea, formed a sort of rough line, and rushed the enemy's trenches. Their magazines were not charged, so they went in with cold steel, and it was over in a minute ... then this race of athletes proceeded to scale the cliffs'.[40] It set the scene for the misrepresentation of the skills and capabilities of the early Diggers. Then Bean fed the public imagining of the Digger as 'the crack shot from the bush, the natural soldier'. Sadly it re-enforced the illusion of the natural soldier in the public mind although the reality was soon striking home to the Diggers.

***

Bean is a towering, complex figure, in the story of the AIF. The twelve-volume official history of WW1 is a masterpiece of social as well as military history. It does however reflect the idiosyncrasies of its author/editor. His record is notable for the scrupulous accuracy in his reporting based on his direct, physical presence on the battlefield (probably no member of the AIF saw more combat than Bean). But he had a propensity to romanticize the Digger that is out of character with his otherwise close focus on reality.

What accounts for this distortion in Bean's otherwise scrupulous reporting? It possibly devolves from a combination of his background and experience. His childhood was spent in semi-rural Bathurst and his youth at an English public school where he was identified as a colonial which likely encouraged his nostalgia for bush-based childhood memories. Then as a young journalist he travelled widely in rural Australia, with his imagination probably stirred by his friendship with the great Australian mythologiser, A.B. (Banjo) Patterson.[41] This background was then re-enforced by his wartime experience.

Two issues stand out. He was a quiet and diffident man who appears to have had difficulty in relating easily with the Diggers. He was essentially an observer and recorder from the background, rather than a seeker of limelight. One biographer describes him as 'idealistic and unworldly, [with] a gentle and unassuming demeanour'.[42] His reserve meant it was probably easier for him to record the facts thereby allowing him to avoid trying to delve into the hearts and minds of the Diggers. When he had been critical it had drawn a savage response that had obviously hurt him. In January 1915 in Egypt, on the instigation of Major General Sir William Bridges, the Divisional Commander, Bean had sent an article home condemning the soldiers' standards in which he said 'there is in the Australian ranks a proportion of men who are uncontrolled, slovenly and in some cases what few Australians can be accused of being – dirty'. The reaction from both officers and men of the Division was savage: there were threats of ostracism or reprisal.[43] He had learned a bitter lesson: it was better to report the actions of the Digger and leave it at that. To avoid the negative did not detract from the objectivity of his reporting.

It was simpler to record the soldiers' valour and to popularise 'the crack shot from the bush' than to highlight their shortcomings. Yet long after the military realised how fallacious the image of the 'natural soldier' was, and had set about rectifying the problem, it remained fixed in the public imagining as a fact and, among some, still does to this day. With the highly Anglophile attitudes of the time there was comfort and pride to be drawn from the image of the concerned citizen leaving the hearth to march to the defence of home, country and empire, laying aside the plough or putting down his tools to take up the equivalent of broadsword, longbow or musket. The war was seen as the chance for the new nation to carve its own niche in a millennium of British military mythology. The crack shot from the bush would take his place alongside those who watched the arrow cloud fall on St Crispin's Day, kneeled at Tilbury as the Queen poured scorn on the Armada, stormed the breach at Badajoz, and rallied to the Colours 'when the Gatling's jammed and the colonel is dead'. Regrettably Australia chose to idealise the wrong features of their hero. He possessed courage, endurance, initiative and adaptability but the one thing he lacked was training. The crack shot from the bush did not have military skill.

***

Turning a civilian into an effective soldier is a precise task. Being 'a crack shot' is but one of his skills. Marksmanship is taught in individual training, the basic tier, before the recruit progresses to higher levels of collective training and eventually to specialist training. The individual battle skills of a soldier are not many; essentially they are fieldcraft, shooting and weapon handling. Beyond these the emphasis in basic training is on developing physical condition and instilling immediate responsiveness to orders, usually achieved, for good or ill, through drill. Yet unfortunately few of the men destined for the infantry battalions of the Australian Corps even had shooting skills.

The infantry were predominantly men from the cities and larger country towns. By 1914 Australia had the distinction of being the most urbanized nation in the world, with 40% of its population living in the six capital cities and most of the rest in large country towns. Despite Bean's image of the crack shot from the bush, even his Official History notes that only 17.3% of soldiers had held rural jobs prior to enlistment.[44] Of these the bulk would have joined the Light Horse regiments that recruited in the rural areas, and they would have served in the Middle East rather than France. The average Digger was no more 'a natural soldier' than his Tommy or Fritz equivalent.

Individual training, as the first step on the ladder, is important. It is however, the next step, collective training, pulling the individuals together into a team and teaching that team how to win its battles, that is crucial. While individual skills are necessary it is by teamwork that battles are won.

This is the most protracted period of training as the soldier is integrated into his section, the section into the platoon, the platoon into the company, the company to the battalion, and so on up the ladder.

***

When the first contingent of the AIF sailed from Albury on 3 November 1914 there was little idea how or where it would be employed. Hence there was no objective on which to focus its collective training. Individual skills continued to be honed, largely under the guidance of ex-British Army NCOs who had enlisted in the AIF. From what can be gleaned from the diaries and records, collective training seems to have largely taken the form of route marches. There seemed a sad absence of developing tactical skills or of getting the men to work together as teams. The consequence of this failure can be seen at Anzac Cove. There was a frightening lack of tactical cohesion in the early days of the campaign. While at the landing there was great dash and élan by many individuals there was a sad absence of unit cohesion. The bold foray of Private Arthur Blackburn of the 10th Battalion, who penetrated deepest into the peninsula, accompanied by a single comrade, reflected great personal courage but also rather reckless behaviour. Two men by themselves could achieve nothing; had their platoon been with them, they could have taken and held that ground.

We conveniently overlook that in the first twenty-four hours the Australians probably outnumbered the Turks in their sector by ten to one.[45] During the early days confusion was a common story. While there was great individual bravery there was also widespread chaos and lack of unit control. Elements of battalions were scattered in small groups all over the beachhead.[46] Some of these groups were advancing while others were retiring. Even individual training proved inadequate with accounts of flustered soldiers leaving their rifles behind in the boats and of many casualties from accidental discharges and misdirected fire.[47] Worse, Bean's diary records reports of between six hundred and a thousand stragglers sheltering near the beach.[48] Gallipoli brought home with a vengeance the weakness of training in the AIF at both the basic and collective levels.

***

A year later there had been a significant change. In July 1916 at Pozieres Blackburn, now a lieutenant, led his company in a succession of four determined attacks to clear several hundred metres of German trench for which he received the VC. Between their withdrawal from Anzac Cove and their deployment to France there had been a sudden urgency to their training. They now recognized their failings and also had a fair idea of what to expect in France and for what they should prepare. To add impetus, their shortcomings were pointed out emphatically by General Sir Archibald Murray, the British commander in Egypt who, to their chagrin, delayed their transfer to France until they had resolved the problem.

The lesson had been learned. In England, where they were centred around Salisbury, they built a comprehensive training structure.[49] Each of the fifteen brigades now had a dedicated training battalion. Specialist corps depots were established. In France there were schools devoted to particular skills both tactical and technical and all were staffed by the most experienced instructors available. This realization of the critical importance of training led to a steady growth in the competence and confidence of the Diggers. Training had become an integral and accepted part of the Corps' activity.

Training was not confined to the rear areas and to formal schools. While in May 1918 there happened to be 2500 officers and men at the Corps or divisional schools, an even greater number were on brigade courses.[50] This training ranged across the gambit of military knowledge from strategy to catering and could take from hours to weeks. Much training was impromptu and could even take place in the front line; for instance, to explain how to operate a captured machine gun or to rehearse a coming patrol.

***

The level of skill they had attained by 1918 through their focus on training is well shown in the cameo battle of Hamel.[51] This was to be the first battle planned by Monash as commander of the Australian corps and it demonstrated his scrupulous planning and attention to detail. Its intent was limited: to nip out a bulge in the line five and a half kilometres wide and to a depth of one and a half kilometres. In doing this they would not only straighten the line but also take high ground, which would make easier any future offensive. Early in the planning two factors arose that were to become features of the battle. Firstly, ten large companies of Americans, who had been training with the Fourth Army, could be available for the attack. Partly in their honour the date for the battle was set for 4th July. Secondly, two battalions of the new Mark 5 tanks would also be available.

***

The initial planning envisaged an attack largely dominated by the tanks, using the techniques that had been successful at Cambrai late the previous year. There the tanks had advanced ahead of the infantry who had followed along behind, essentially left to mop-up. So as not to constrain the tanks' manoeuvre there had been no creeping barrage. The Australians were skeptical that it was a winning tactic. They had little confidence in tanks after their experience at Bullecourt in April 1917, where the Mark I tanks had failed to arrive, leaving the 4th Division to attack alone, with neither

Monash (seated) with his staff. Tom Blamey, Chief of Staff, directly behind him. Walter Coxen, his CRA, on the far right. Source: AWM E02750

tank nor artillery support and, in consequence, it had suffered severely. Major General Ewen Sinclair-MacLagan, commander of 4th Division and who was to command the attack, wanted the tanks and infantry to fight together, but under the control of the infantry. Monash agreed and convinced the tank commander. Then his two senior staff officers, Brigadier-General Thomas Blamey, the chief of staff, and Brigadier-General Walter Coxen, commander of the Corps artillery, insisted the infantry must be protected by a creeping barrage. The plan was evolving, but differently than had been initially envisaged.

To overcome the Australian's lack of trust in the tanks a program of familiarization and joint training was conducted over the weeks preceding the battle that established both confidence and mutual respect. The infantry found the new Mark 5 tank could keep pace with them and was much more reliable and manoeuvrable than the Mark I. It was also better armoured and less likely to fall prey to German anti-tank rifles. Through demonstrations, displays and rehearsals a strong bond was established. During this time the principles of infantry/tank co-operation were established that is still current. The Corps was not only training but devising the doctrine where there was the need.

Everything was as precise, systematic and logical as the staff could make it. The ten assault battalions were from three brigades, one each of the 2nd, 3rd and 4th Divisions, and were all placed under the command of Major General Sinclair-MacLagan, whose 4th Division lay opposite the objective. This allocation would both spread the experience as widely as possible through the Corps and also, by using brigades convenient to the objective, minimize movement and risks to security.

***

Two conferences, each of half a day duration were held, one with an agenda of 118 issues, the second with 133. This was an attention to detail that was in marked contrast to Gallipoli and the early days on the Western Front. Yet the best laid plans can be disrupted by external demands. General John Pershing, the American commander, intervened, believing the US troops insufficiently trained for battle. Six of the ten companies were withdrawn. At the last moment his headquarters realized there were a remaining four, and demanded they too be withdrawn. By that stage they were in their assembly area and their removal would have required a total re-structure of the plan. Monash refused. It was too late to release them and, if they went, the battle would not proceed. Haig concurred, and the Americans remained.

The Corps artillery was supplemented by a further six brigades (or regiments in current parlance) of field guns and two of heavy artillery. Over the preceding weeks it had been customary for the artillery to drop harassing fire of gas, smoke and high-explosives on the German defences for an hour from 3 am. When this ritual began on the morning of 4th July it filled three purposes. It covered the noise of the sixty tanks moving from their assembly area a mile back to the start-line. In response to the gas shells the Germans had become accustomed to donning their gas masks, and did so on the morning of the 4th, and fought in them to their discomfort, although no gas was fired that morning. The smoke also masked the objective from German observation, leaving their commanders unsure of what was happening, and thereby making the customary counter-attacks difficult to plan or launch.

***

The harassing fire at 3 am fell as always in depth but the range was gradually shortened until the shells were falling where the creeping barrage for the attack would begin. Then at 3.10 am, H Hour, the full barrage crashed down, with the shells of the field guns falling 200 metres from the start line, those of the howitzers a further 200 metres out and those of the medium and heavy guns yet a further 200 metres. The infantrymen of the ten assaulting battalions, together with their four attached US companies, rose from where they had waited at the forming-up place and began their advance with the tanks towards the barrage, which after four minutes began its progressive shifts.

It was not yet dawn and initially their way was lighted by the flashes of the shells of the barrage. They were attacking to the east, but even as the sun rose the dust of the barrage and the smoke of the harassing fire saved them from being dazzled and moreover the German positions were silhouetted by the rising sun against the mist of smoke and dust.

***

The complexity of battle is always so great that despite all the best effort, and regardless of the skill and training of the force, it is inevitable that something will go wrong. There is a famous military dictum that states that 'no plan lasts beyond the first shot'. Yet Hamel went extraordinarily well. There were the inevitable errors – a battery of guns was not properly registered and in consequence a battalion advanced sandwiched between the barrage to its front, while the shells of the recalcitrant battery fell behind it.

Their primitive communications meant commanders customarily lost control of the battle once the troops crossed the start-line. Hamel, though, was planned in such finite detail that Monash had a good idea of what should be happening. He had predicted the battle would last 90 minutes: it took 93. Once begun, neither he nor Sinclair-MacLagan could effectively influence its course, but at least through the careful planning they had a better idea of where their troops should be. It must be recognized that it was a minor battle by the standards of WW1, with comparatively few participants and with limited objectives. It cost the Australian Corps 1400 casualties, but they achieved all their objectives, took 1600 German prisoners and captured 1700 machine-guns. Yet even the Diggers were frustrated that, having broken in so easily, they were not allowed to go on and take the German gun lines. That triumph was to be reserved for their next battle.

***

Much was learned, new methods were trialled, and concepts were tested. The infantry and tanks working together was proven to be a battle-winning combination. Three important factors about the tanks were now recognized by the Diggers. They could suppress the fire of the German machine-guns, they could clear paths through the barbed-wire by compressing it, and their improved armour allowed them to operate very close to the barrage. Where at Cambrai the tanks and guns had been carefully kept apart, now at Hamel it had been shown the two could work closely together- and so they would henceforth. The tanks could now be integrated into the combined-arms team to work with both the infantry and the guns. The Diggers were no longer skeptics.

Of lesser glamour but equal importance were the lessons learned of battle administration: resupply and casualty evacuation. A form of air re-supply, with planes dropping ammunition by parachute to the advancing infantry, proved successful. For the first-time carrier tanks brought forward the 'consolidation stores' of barbed wire, pickets, picks, shovels and ammunition that would otherwise have been the load of 1200 infantry acting as porters. This enabled the infantry, who having reached their objective, to more quickly prepare their defences against the inevitable German counter attacks. The carrier tanks then back-loaded the casualties so quickly that special arrangements had to be improvised to then have them evacuated speedily from the battle zone. A number of ideas were coming together at last into an integrated whole; the concept of the combined-arms battle was evolving.

***

Hamel was a small battle with limited objectives but several factors made it stand out. It drew attention as it was the first successful attack by the allies since the start of the German Spring Offensive in March. Its planning presaged a new and different approach to battle. New techniques were being introduced onto the battlefield that could change the course of the war and neutralize the superiority of the German defence. Other tried and proven techniques were being integrated and their effect in combination was far greater than in isolation. On the following Sunday the elderly French President, Georges Clemenceau, came to the headquarters of the 4th Division to thank the Australian Corps.

The battle reflected the dramatic change that the Australian military had undergone in the three years from 25 April 1915. In that short time they had transformed into a highly professional, skilled and superbly trained force. Their competence was now apparent at many levels: the skills of the individual soldiers; their teamwork; and their mastery of the planning, preparation and conduct of complex operations. They showed themselves to be free-thinkers and innovators and, while many of the techniques had been devised by others, they had the imagination to take those ideas, refine them and then to integrate them effectively into the battle-plan. Importantly this was not just the exclusive preserve of Monash and the senior officers but extended throughout the ranks of the Corps. Hamel may have been a small battle but its innovations made it significant for what would follow. The scene was set to apply this package of new tactics and techniques on a larger stage.

***

While the Australian Corps had launched the first small step in the allied counter-offensive it is the French who claim the decisive opening move. The French had suffered a succession of German attacks in the final gasp of the Spring Offensive and had been driven back to the Marne. There they rallied and retaliated with a determined counter-attack on 18 July in which 24 French divisions supported by 2000 guns and 500 tanks pushed the Germans back ten kilometres. In the coming Hundred Days the French armies, together with the bulk of the American divisions, paralleled the advance of the BEF and drove the Germans back to the frontier. What was lacking in finesse was made up with stolid determination and, at last, overwhelming numbers.

CHAPTER 5

The Battle of Amiens I

'Fighters not soldiers'

Battlecraft

Fellers of Australier,
Cobbers, chaps an' mates,
Hear the bloody enemy
Kickin' at the gates!
Blow the bloody bugle,
Beat the bloody drum,
Upper-cut and out the cow
To kingdom bloody come!

Get a bloody move on,
Have some bloody sense,
Learn the bloody art of
Self de-bloody-fence.

C.J. Dennis[52]

In essence the tactical concept for Amiens was of a surprise frontal attack in depth sufficient to over-run all German defences and its artillery. For the concept to succeed required the application of a number of battlecraft techniques, particularly in the methods of artillery fire, infantry maneuver and tank support and for the integration of these techniques into a unified combined-arms battle plan. The success of the tactics hinged on the battlecraft skills that had evolved and then been tried and tested at Hamel. Success also depended on having the right equipment for the job: particularly reliable artillery shells, tanks with adequate armour and a mass of light machine-guns. At Amiens these components came together. The battlecraft, weaponry and tactics at last matched and clicked into place.

Battlecraft, also known as minor-tactics, is the name given to the fusion of a number of collective skills of the soldier. They include such fundamentals as handling crew-served weapons, battle drills, section and platoon formations, obstacle crossing, target indication and fire control. They are the skills taught in the first stage of collective training that integrate the soldiers into the team and gets them all working together. It is a crucial step in establishing combat effectiveness. Sound battlecraft, linked with good junior leadership, and high morale allows that team to dominate its piece of the battlefield. Over the course of the preceding three years of war the skills attained by the infantry, the gunners, tank crews, airmen, engineers and by all the other components of the BEF had reached a high level. Their competence was now displayed at the Battle of Amiens. And it was the battlecraft of the Diggers which set a benchmark. The men of the Australian Corps had become among the most competent soldiers in the BEF. It was the Australians, together with the other dominion contingents, who were now invariably chosen for the most challenging tasks. Together with a handful of British divisions they were essentially the 'shock troops' of the BEF, despite Haig's denial of such an elite.[53].

There is then irony to be seen in the refusal of some senior British officers to recognize them even as soldiers. Bean records a prevailing attitude among some that 'these men might make fighters, perhaps, but soldiers never'[54]. Besides its condescension it reflected elements of both a truth and a delusion. It is a criticism justified by their performance in the early days on Gallipoli, but that had been corrected by intense training, particularly collective training, and the honing of their skills. The delusion lay in the belief that the semi-feudal system of the British Army, with its class-based structure, reflected the pinnacle of soldiering and that it was a model that should be emulated by the Australians.

There is no disputing that the British Army was the mentor of the AIF. The AIF was modelled on the British Army and it was guided in its formation and early years by seconded British officers and an invaluable rump of ex-British NCOs and warrant officers who had migrated pre-war to Australia. British systems and methods were accepted unquestioningly, right down to the mincing thirty-inch marching pace. Yet despite the effort to make it a clone of the British Army there was one great difference that would frustrate that intent. Over the preceding century, since the arrival of the First Fleet, a very different social system had evolved in Australia. It was an egalitarian society with its own attitudes to discipline and social hierarchy which was reflected in the AIF. The leadership style and the approach to discipline that was required could never mirror that of the class-ridden British Army of 1914. In consequence one of the great attributes of the AIF was that the Digger was a thinking soldier. Most armies of that vintage preferred their soldiers to be automatons, instinctively obedient and unquestioningly responsive. The Digger brought a different background to his service. He was used to having an opinion and expressing it, and uniquely among armies of the time, this was encouraged in the AIF.

The disdain of a clutch of senior British officers at the initial incompetence of the Australians morphed into irritation as their skills improved. By late 1917 the fighting quality of the Digger was more than equal of that of the average Tommy. The Digger was being noticed and this was compounded by his natural conspicuousness. He was often loud, brash and self-confident. He also stood out physically, being on the average, taller and more lanky than his Tommy counterpart. He was also identifiable by his uniform. With its voluminous pockets it lacked the neatness of the British service-dress, but it was warm, comfortable and practicable and the Diggers were proud of it. It was the product of the Commonwealth Government Clothing Factory fortuitously established in 1912 in South Melbourne. Soldiers pay great attention to their 'gear': their clothing, boots, packs and 'webbing' are very important to them as they confer what little comfort he can find in the field. The Diggers approved of what was provided: it was superior in design and quality to that of the Tommies', but that made it a further target of envy and criticism. And, above all, it was his hat that made him most distinctive. His slouch hat kept off rain and sun but also stood out very distinctly. It could be worn smartly with the left side clipped up, chin strap on the point of the chin, a polished buckle level with the mouth, or it could be seen worn any other way, to being a hat tipped on the back of the head, with a drunken leer beneath.

***

On 26 July 1918 Foch issued the formal order for the operation which was 'to disengage Amiens and the Amiens–Paris railway'. At the same time he placed the adjoining French First Army under Haig's command for the operation. This left a scant two weeks to complete the planning, deploy the forces, and prepare for the attack. Such now was the skill of the staff at the many levels of command, and the responsiveness of the forces, that it was easily achieved. Rawlinson's Fourth Army was to attack together with the French First Army on its right. The Australian Corps was to be central in Fourth Army with the British III Corps on its left, on the north bank of the Somme and the Canadian Corps on its right, with that boundary delineated by the Amiens–Nesle railway line.[55]

To the front of Fourth Army were six divisions of the German Second Army deployed in three belts of defence. Behind them were a further six divisions in reserve. The initial assault was to be by seven divisions: two each British and Australian and three Canadian. This meant far less than the desired ratio for the attack of 3:1. However, the German divisions were under-strength, improving the ratio in terms of manpower to a more acceptable 5:3. Still, it showed a confidence within the BEF that had not existed previously. It is a military convention that a formation is attacked by the next sized formation: that a battalion position is assaulted by a brigade, and a brigade by a division. At Amiens two Australian attacking divisions would be pitted against two German defending divisions.

By the end of the day the Germans had lost 27,000, including 15,750 POW of whom 7,920 had been taken by the Australians. Taken too were over 400 German guns. It was conceded in the official German Monograph as 'the greatest defeat which the German Army suffered since the beginning of the war'. The cost to the Australians was 652 casualties of whom 83 were killed. It was a stunning victory. It is worth examining how it was achieved against the conventional odds.

***

Surprise. Strategy in WW1 had been bereft of subtlety. The Gallipoli landings had been signalled months in advance. The great offensives had usually been well advertised, by up to a week of preliminary bombardment, allowing ample time for the Germans to marshal reserves and re-enforcements. Amiens opened a whole new spectrum. Suddenly surprise and its component parts of secrecy and deception re-appeared in military thinking. Interestingly recent British Army analysis of 160 land campaigns of the 20th century showed that if the attackers had surprise, air superiority and aggressive ground reconnaissance there was a 95% probability of success.[56] All these factors were present at Amiens.

The Germans were deceived into complacency on the Amiens front. To demonstrate a focus on defence the Australian Corps extended its front southward, taking over six kilometres of trenches that had been held by the French, and were then seen to be deepening them, as if intent on static warfare. Yet it was from these trenches the Canadians would attack. It was vital that the Canadians, who had been in reserve, not be seen in the vicinity of Amiens. The presence of both Dominion corps together would have given a clear signal of a pending offensive. The Canadians sent two battalions, two casualty clearing stations and signals detachments north to broadcast a Canadian presence in Flanders. For the rest, strict limits were set on who could be told of the coming attack and only two days before the assault were the Canadians moved to the vicinity of Amiens. It succeeded; the Germans were astonished when the Canadians appeared out of the morning mist on 8 August.

Secrecy was critical if surprise was to be achieved. From the plateau of the Santerre the German forward defences overlooked the low ground on which Amiens lay. It was there that Fourth Army had to marshal all the forces and resources for the attack and to do it without it being seen by the Germans. Into an area approximately ten kilometres square had to be crowded over 500 tanks together with their crews and fuel, hundreds of extra guns and 700,000 shells, three cavalry divisions with their thousands of horses, and, eventually, two days before the assault, the four large divisions of the Canadian Corps. To deploy and conceal this mass was a seemingly impossible task, yet it was achieved.

All movement was at night. The roads were spread with sand to reduce the noise. Iron-bound wheels were wound with rope. Bombers were flown overhead to drown the noise of tank movement. A dawn reconnaissance was flown to check the camouflage. What little the forward German troops saw or heard and reported was not believed at their headquarters. An attack on 31 July by 8th Brigade to straighten the line for the incoming British III Corps drew a retaliatory German pre-dawn attack on 6 August that took 200 British prisoners. Earlier, on 4 August, five Diggers in a post in the recently occupied old French trenches were seized in a German raid. There were fears any could reveal the plan, but none did so. The reticence of the Diggers was even held up by German intelligence to their own troops as a model of resisting interrogation should they be taken prisoner.

The guns too played their part in the surprise. As at Hamel there was no preliminary bombardment. The opening of the barrage signalled the start of the assault. And when in the preceding days German gun positions were identified they were silently registered. If a German gun was relocated, fire continued on the vacated site even if the new position had been identified.

Several factors were to the advantage of Fourth Army. Amiens had been cleared of its civilian population during the Spring Offensive and, as it had been under intermittent shelling since, had not been re-occupied. This reduced the ever-present chance of German spies observing and reporting the build-up. Secondly, several days of cloudy weather hampered German aerial reconnaissance. The new, or more exactly rediscovered, tactic of surprise worked perfectly: so much so that Amiens became a model for its use in the next war. When the 3,532 French and British guns thundered at 4.20 am on 8 August it was to the astonishment of the Germans

***

The Guns. WW1 was the 'gunners' war' and Amiens 'a gunners' battle'.[57] The guns dominated the war and played the major part in its battles. It was 'the monstrous anger of the guns' that inflicted the bulk of the carnage on men and materiel. The effect of the large scything lumps of metal was catastrophic: men slashed in two, heads detached, bodies blown to smithereens, often nothing left but a red spray, and a landscape churned into a morass.

Artillery, more than the other arms, had entered the war with a Napoleonic mind-set and left it as the most technologically and scientifically attuned arm. The pre-war image was of guns being galloped into action to bore holes in serried ranks of charging infantry, or of huge siege guns dragged into position to batter down the walls of the enemy stronghold. The realities of the battlefield led to re-evaluation and eventually the gunners came to recognize that their role was not to destroy either men or walls, but to neutralize. It required a major mental re-adjustment for the gunners to accept that their purpose was to make the enemy keep his head down.

In the early battles thousands of tons of shells had been dumped on German positions in an effort to obliterate their defences before the battle began. This was never achieved: the dug-outs were too deep, the guns too inaccurate, the wire too thick, and the barrage gave sufficient warning of impending attack for reserves to be deployed in anticipation. Through experience the gunners came to realize that a single field gun firing four shells a minute could neutralize 25 metres of trench-line, forcing the enemy to take cover. This in turn meant the infantry, if they followed closely behind the barrage, could 'jump' the trench before the Germans could get their heads up. Equivalently, in counter-battery fire, if the shelling was sustained at the same rate of four shells per minute on a gun-pit, it could keep that gun from being fired for as long as the shelling lasted.

Acceptance of the role of neutralization was a breakthrough. It could only work, however, if the guns could put shells where they were meant to be. The infantry have always belittled the gunners with the title 'drop shorts'. As the war progressed there was increasing emphasis on getting the shells in the right place. The range of each gun is different because of barrel-wear. New methods of 'calibration' allowed each gun to be separately adjusted. Meteorological conditions; air pressure, wind and rain could all affect the fall of shot and had to be taken into consideration. Weather forecasting was elevated to a science. It was also crucial to know precisely where the gun, as well as its target, was located. Hence there were strides in cartography to provide accurate maps, and in surveying, to be sure the gun was where it was thought to be. These developments meant that when the guns fired there was a high degree of confidence that the shells would fall where intended. This allowed 'silent registration', obviating the need for ranging shots, thereby keeping secret the knowledge of the location of a target until the battle started. Neutralizing the enemy guns meant their location had to be fixed.

Techniques of flash-spotting, sound ranging and aerial photography were developed, in which two Australians, famous in other fields, played major parts: the Nobel physicist Lawrence Braggs[58], with sound ranging, and the Artic explorer Hubert Wilkins, with aerial photography.

For Amiens the guns of Fourth Army were doubled to 2000, half of which were 18 pounder field guns, which together with 300 4.5 inch howitzers, were allocated to the barrage to clear the way for the infantry in the first of the three phases of the battle. This meant sufficient field guns for the fire of one gun per 22 metres of front, better than the prescribed minimum of 25 metres per gun. The opening barrage at 4.20 am fell 200 metres beyond the infantry start-line, with the shells of the heavier 4.5-inch howitzers falling a further 200 metres ahead. Then after three minutes it advanced 100 metres for a further three minutes. And so the pattern continued with 40 lifts over two and a half hours with the time on each bound slowly increasing to allow for tiring infantry. The high explosive shells with instantaneous fuzes enabled the infantry to move within twenty-five metres of the wall of fire – 'leaning on the barrage' as Bean described it.

The first phase carried the leading two Australian divisions 3.2 kilometres, through the established German defences and into his rear areas. It was the extremity of the range of the field guns, and it was also the rear boundary of the zone in which the German field guns had been located. Some of the field guns then had to be quickly brought forward for the next phase. There was then no longer need for a barrage as the reserve brigades of the two German divisions facing the Australians were widely dispersed: nor, without careful preparation, could a further barrage be brought down with guaranteed accuracy. Consequently individual guns were designated to go forward with the infantry to fire over open sights at targets of opportunity, and artillery forward observers accompanied the infantry to call gun fire onto distant targets.

All the medium and heavy artillery, nearly half the guns, had been allocated to the counter-battery fire tasks. The sound ranging, flash spotting and aerial photography had identified the location of 504 of the 540 German guns in the Fourth Army zone. Few of these guns fired a shell on 8 August: muzzle caps were still on many as they were over-run by the advancing infantry and the German gunners were still cowering in their bunkers.

Amiens saw the culmination of a number of developments in artillery.

There was no single new innovation on display, rather it was the battle that reflected the integration of a host of developments that had evolved over the preceding year. In that twelve months there had been a transformation in warfare. No longer did the infantry and guns fight a separate battle and there was new confidence and trust between the two arms. That the infantry were now prepared to come so close to the barrage reflected both their faith in the gunners and the maturity of their battlecraft.

***

The Infantry. The 2nd and 3rd Divisions led the way. Each attacked with two brigades forward, and each brigade with two battalions 'up'. These eight leading Australian infantry battalions that crossed their start-line at 4.20 am on 8 August and advanced into the fog were very different from the battalions that had landed at Anzac Cove four years earlier. Then, each had deployed around a thousand men, now they went into battle with between 250 and 350. Those battalions which had fought at Gallipoli had rebuilt, sometimes seven times over, since 1915 but still their numbers were depleted. Casualties and the tail-off in recruiting had taken its toll. Although battalion strength was usually in the vicinity of 400–500 this was not what they took into battle. Absent were the 'sick, lame and halt', those at schools and courses, and those deliberately 'left out of battle', the 10% who were potential leaders, who would provide the nucleus around which to rebuild if the battalion was decimated. Rifle companies 200 strong in 1915 were now lucky to have 80 men.

Numbers however meant less in 1918. There was now a recognition that it was firepower rather than bayonets that counted. Monash had remarked that as long as a battalion had thirty Lewis guns it was effective.[59] The glue of the 1918 Australian battalion was its firepower and its cohesion. The men knew each other well. It seems re-enforcements were ;quickly integrated into the team. There was no exclusion of 'the new chums'; they were welcomed, and indeed most were old members returning after recuperation from wounds or sickness. A high 80% of those wounded eventually returned. It can be speculated too that, despite Napoleon's aphorism, God is not necessarily on the side of the big battalions. A small group of men with confidence in each other could outfight a larger force which lacks cohesion. Firepower and teamwork is the key to victory.

The men recognized their interdependence: there was undoubtedly the odd 'bit of biff' in the estaminets as tensions and 'pecking-order' were resolved, but the unity among the Diggers in the last year of the war stands out clearly. Where at Gallipoli the horror had been largely faced by the individual alone as a personal challenge, by Amiens there was a realization that survival depended on mateship and team work. There seems little doubt that it was the sharing of the horror that gave the young men the strength to continue to 'jump the bags' or 'go over the top' again and again. The battalion team was now the Digger's life, and he was prepared to put his life at risk for that team.

Amiens displayed the skill and confidence the infantry had acquired. As an example: consider the responsibility on the shoulders of the young battalion intelligence officers who, after dark on 7 August, had gone forward with their teams of two or three intelligence duty-men and found their way carefully to their respective battalion 'forming-up places'. It was there, just behind the forward trenches, that their battalions would shake out into their assault formations. Using compass bearings and pacing, they laid out the tapes and markers for the troops. It had to be done with great accuracy and in the pitch dark. A battalion mis-positioned could cause chaos to its neighbours and jeopardize the attack.

Battle is exhausting. The tension and the terror saps physical energy. Not only were these men going into action but the tactical concept demanded an attack over a considerable distance of 8.3 kilometres from the forward defences to the final objective. The Fourth Army had laid down three phases for the attack. The first phase, to the Green Line, was about 3.2 kilometres; the second, to the Red Line, was 4.8 kilometres; and finally a short hop of around half a kilometre to the final objective, the Blue Line. The Australian plan called for different formations to be used for each phase. The Australian sector was neatly delineated. Its left flank was the south bank of the Somme: its right flank was the Amiens–Nesle railway line. This provided a frontage of 6.6 kilometres which gradually expanded to 8.3 kilometres.

The staff, recognizing the importance of keeping the troops as fresh as possible, balanced the distances they had to move in each phase as best they could manage. Hence the Australian Corps undertook the complex manoeuvre that is known as 'passage of lines' where one formation leapfrogs another. The assembly area for the 2nd and 3rd Divisions which would open the attack was about three kilometres behind the forward trenches. They would then move to the forming-up place just behind the forward trenches and at H Hour leapfrog the two forward divisions. At the start of the second phase they in turn would be leapfrogged by the 4th and 5th Divisions which would attack through to the Red Line where their reserve brigades would pass through, repeating the process to advance to the final Blue Line. Passage of Lines can be a risky manoeuvre where inexperienced troops can become confused and units entangled. It is rarely done by large formations and its use at Amiens reflected the confidence of the commanders in the experience of their troops. The confidence was justified as it went without a hitch and thereby spread the load of distance to be travelled more equitably.

Between 1 and 2 am the 2nd and 3rd Divisions came forward and the troops were led to their locations where they lay down, mostly in the recently harvested stubble to await dawn. Some likely dozed while others, on their backs, may have watched the stars till the mist rose. There may have been quiet conversations but probably most were alone with their thoughts. All would have been hoping fervently that they would achieve surprise and would have been concerned when German shells began to fall on the right flank brigade. It did not last long but left 20 casualties. Nothing could be done but for them to lie there exposed and receive it. It transpired it was pre-programmed fire in support of a raid by the Germans on the forward trenches which they found empty, but failed to relate to a likely attack.

Around 4 am, while a bomber circled noisily overhead, the tanks lumbered forward and were guided through the reclining infantry into their positions near the forward edge of the forming-up place. The infantry would have watched their arrival with relief. A close bond had been established with the crews of the tanks allocated to the battalions.

Just as the gunners had learned that their mission was to neutralize, so too the infantry now accepted that their role was simply 'to take and hold ground'. Realization brought new ways of employing the infantry and new demands on the staff to support it. It was Monash who recognized that the infantry should 'advance under the maximum possible array of mechanical resources – guns, machine guns, tanks, mortars and aeroplanes'.[60] At last there was acceptance that firepower should clear the way for the infantry to reach and occupy their objective. Masses of infantry, advancing shoulder to shoulder, were no longer needed to clear the battlefield. This was now the responsibility of the 'mechanical resources'. The task of the infantry, as the gunners like to describe it, was now 'to follow the barrage and bayonet the wounded'.

At Passchendaele it had been considered necessary to attack with a density of six infantrymen to each metre of front. Hamel had then been fought successfully using a new criteria of one man per metre. Now at Amiens where the assault was by eight battalions on a frontage of six kilometres, the density was even less. Battalions were attacking on frontages of slightly less than a kilometre. It was a new way of fighting. Battles would now be won by superior fire-power rather than massed bayonets.

When the 2000 guns of Fourth Army fired at 4.20 am on the morning of 8 August the men of the leading Australian assault battalions clambered to their feet, admired the heavy mist that limited visibility to twenty metres, lit their pipes or cigarettes, and moved off quickly to catch up with the barrage falling 200 metres ahead of them. They moved now, not in extended waves as they had in the battles in Flanders, but in section files. At Amiens each leading platoon had its 'own' tank in close support. Hugging the barrage, 'leaning on the fire', they advanced. Where the guns or their tank failed to neutralize a German machine gun before it could be 'jumped' by the Diggers, it was assaulted using their own resources. The direct fire of their Lewis guns would keep German heads down while rifle grenades were dropped on those heads. Meanwhile, under this covering fire, an assault group would manoeuvre close enough to finish the business. Fire power had become important to the infantry. The thirty Lewis guns per battalion now formed the core around which it fought.

The other feature of the 1918 Digger, which stands in contrast to the earlier years, is his agility. No longer was he loaded down with heavy packs, or picks and shovels. They carried only the essentials for battle: their weapon, 120 rounds of ammunition, two grenades, two water bottles, iron rations and gas mask and cape. The experienced soldier knew his life depended on the speed of his reaction and to be encumbered risked his life and that of his mates.

The assault rolled forward. A succession of lines of defence of the forward German brigades and then the pits of their field artillery were over-run and, by around 7.20 am, the First Objective, the Green Line, was reached and the two leading divisions began to dig in. At 8 am the fog lifted. Many commentators remarked on the extraordinary scene that was revealed. As far as the eye could see were men and tanks steadily advancing or consolidating their new position, while teams of horses were 'galloping forward' the field artillery. There was everywhere a sense of purpose and positive activity that had been lacking at this stage in most previous battles.

At 8.20 the 4th and 5th Divisions passed through in their passage of lines and took the lead for the next phase. As the First Phase had seen the major German defences and their field guns over-run there was no longer need for a creeping barrage. The defences of the reserve German brigades were widely dispersed and centred on copses and villages and on these, and the previously located German medium gun positions, the artillery now concentrated its fire. Some of the field guns that had been brought forward were allocated to the assaulting battalions and moved with them to provide direct fire on troublesome German positions. Only half the Mark 5 tanks had accompanied the first phase, and they were now joined by the rest. This mass of tanks, moving about a hundred metres ahead of the infantry, provided some of the protection previously afforded by the barrage.

Movement over the five kilometres to the Second Objective was rapid. When delayed by German machine guns, smoke from shells or bombs were used to screen the movement of the assault. In the previous weeks whenever smoke had been fired it had been accompanied by gas shells. The Germans had become accustomed to donning their gas masks at the sight of smoke and continued to do so, thereby inhibiting their fighting ability. A gas mask is a cumbersome and suffocating piece of equipment in which to fight.

On the right flank the 5th Division advanced over rolling terrain, seized the village of Harbonnieres, and elements began to reach the Second Objective, the Red Line, by 10 am. On the left the 4th Division, flanking the Somme, made slower progress, slowed down by the need to clear the re-entrants and gullies of the river. On the north bank of the Somme the British III Corps, after completing its First Phase, had been halted by the Germans. This left the Chipilly spur, with German machine-guns and artillery threatening the flank of 4th Division. It was from the enfilade fire from Chipilly that the Australian Corps suffered its heaviest casualties for the day. It managed, however, to consolidate by 11 am on the Red Line, and both divisions then sent forward their reserve brigades, between one and two kilometres, to the final objective, the Blue Line, the old Amiens trench line of previous year's battle. To the right of the Australians the Canadians and, further to their right, the French were both on their objectives by mid-day. Seldom in previous battles had the final objectives ever been reached.

***

Armour. For the battle the Australian Corps had been allocated 108 Mark 5 tanks. Of these nearly half accompanied the 2nd and 3rd Divisions in the First Phase. This provided a tank in support of each leading platoon. The Mark 5 was a significantly better tank than the Mark 1 which had failed the 4th Division at Bullecourt in the previous year. Weighing nearly 30 tonnes, with a 150 horse-power engine it was capable of moving at 7.5 kilometres an hour. Its eight man crew served the two 57-mm cannon and four machine-guns or, in the 'female' version, no cannon but eight machine-guns.

The tanks had 'married up' with their respective battalions, and in many cases had that battalion's tactical sign painted on its hull. With each tank travelled a scout of the platoon to direct the attention of the half-blind tank to the concerns of the infantry. Despite the swirling mist and the clamour of the barrage of the First Phase the combination generally worked well. The barrage concealed and shielded the tanks from the German guns. The tanks silenced those German machine-guns not neutralized by the artillery. In the intense battle of the First Phase, as the infantry fought their way through the primary German defences and over-ran the German field artillery, the tanks played a vital role grinding a path through the wire obstacles, and as moving strong-points were able, at close quarters, to lay down covering fire.

In the Second Phase, after the mist had lifted, and the assault was into the German rear areas, the role of the tanks changed. As the reserve tanks were released there were now double the number, and over the open ground, on which there was no creeping barrage, the tanks led the way, 100 metres and more in front of the infantry. However, those few German guns not located and neutralized by the counter-battery program now took a heavy toll. At this stage in their development, the tanks had yet to recognize the importance of moving by bounds, under the cover of the fire of other tanks. At Amiens they operated singly, without the mutual support, and were vulnerable. The tank losses were heavy. Fourth Army had begun the day with a total of 415 tanks, both Mark 5 and Whippet light tanks. Of these 270 were lost, some by ditching and mechanical failure but most to German guns and anti-tank rifles. The fields were dotted with blazing pyres. They had however, played a valiant and vital role in helping 4th and 5th Divisions through to their Second Phase objective.

Two derivatives of the Mark 5 then played their part in the Third phase, the advance to the Blue Line. The Mark 5* (star) was an elongated version with interior space to carry 14 passengers. The 4th and 5th Divisions were each allocated 18 of these embryonic 'armoured personnel carriers' with the intent of moving the Lewis and Vickers teams forward. Their fumes, heat, noise and vibration made them so uncomfortable that in most instances the infantry chose to walk. Although as a personnel carrier they were not a great success they offered valuable covering fire while the infantry consolidated on the Blue Line.

Infantry is most vulnerable after it has seized its objective and is adjusting from attack to the defence on the ground it has taken. At this point they are tired, their numbers and ammunition depleted, and they have no prepared defences against a determined counter-attack. For the infantry to have carried with them all the picks and shovels and defence stores needed to secure the objective would have overburdened them. These items had been

Armoured cars on the Peronne Road preparing to break out in the German rear areas.
Source: AWM E03099

previously been carried forward by porters drawn from reserve battalions, who had to move through barrages the enemy deliberately dropped to prevent their passage. Now there were new flat-bed carrier tanks onto which the consolidation stores could be loaded, each carrying an equivalent load of 200 men. The Corps had 36 carrier tanks allocated and they brought not only the stores and ammunition but also hot meals and water and took back the wounded. While they get scant reference in the records, to the infantry they must have seemed a miraculous innovation.

Some have suggested Amiens saw the genesis of blitzkrieg. This is hardly so. The role of the tank was limited to the protection and support of the infantry. There was no perception of the tanks breaking through into the rear areas: that remained the province of the cavalry, in anticipation of which all the British cavalry had been deployed to Amiens.

There was one armoured vehicle, the armoured car, which shone a light on the future. The old Roman Road bisected the Australian front. With the completion of the First Phase, a battalion of 14 armoured cars stormed along the road and, four kilometres beyond the final objective, fanned-out to left and right into the German rear areas. These Austins, capable of 42 km/h in both forward and reverse, and armed with machine-guns in two rotatable turrets, created chaos in the German rear areas, shooting-up depots, ammunition dumps, gun lines, advancing re-enforcements and, most significantly, headquarters, in one of which was seized the detailed plan of the Hindenburg Line that later was to be of crucial importance in another Australian attack. One by one the cars were knocked out but their success had shown the potential of fast, well protected armoured vehicles.

**

The Cavalry. Wherever there was the whiff of a chance of a breakthrough Haig would deploy his cavalry 'just in case'. Hence all three British cavalry divisions were at Amiens. A brigade was assigned to the Australian Corps and did valiant work in the Second Phase, galloping ahead of 5th Division until stopped, as always, by the German machine-guns, but not before capturing the very large railway gun that had for months fired its 302-kilogram shells 25 kilometres into Amiens. Its barrel is now displayed on the lawns of the Australian War Memorial in Canberra.

Amiens saw a futile attempt to integrate the old and new: linked to each cavalry division was a battalion of Whippet light tanks, there to suppress the German machine-guns. The Whippet was too fast though for a trotting horse and, with a top speed of around 12 kilometres per hour, far too slow for cavalry at the gallop. The linkage came quickly unstuck and the carcasses of a thousand horses littered the battlefield.

***

Air. In the days preceding 8 August allied air strength had been built up for the battle. Aircraft had played an important part in achieving the surprise with which the attack was launched, keeping the skies over Amiens clear of German planes, helping spot the German guns and providing noise to cover the night movement of the tanks. On the morning of 8 August there were 626 British and 1104 French aircraft available to support the battle and only 365 opposing German machines. Although it was a late start, waiting for the fog to lift, they gave valuable support during the Second and Third phases, attacking German strong points that were delaying the advance, or blinding them with smoke bombs to allow the infantry and tanks to close. Their close support included keeping the headquarters informed of the progress by dropping marked maps affixed to streamers, providing aerial re-supply of ammunition and, most importantly, keeping the Fokkers away. As the Third Phase was completed their attention was switched to the Somme bridges to try to prevent either German withdrawal or re-enforcement. Hitting a bridge with an iron bomb has always been a difficult task and the Somme bridges proved indestructible. Over the next few days, as German aircraft numbers increased, so did the intensity of the air battle over the Somme: the RAF lost 44 aircraft and a further 52 were badly damaged.

***

The Engineers. The flat and open nature of the Santerre Plateau demanded little from the engineers in support of the battle. Hence they were able to concentrate their resources on the vital Roman Road that bisected the Australian Corps' area of operations. The road was very conveniently located. Along it could race the armored cars to break out behind the German lines. It enabled the quick evacuation of casualties and the rapid movement of urgently needed stores and equipment to the front. Here the engineers played their part, filling craters, removing fallen trees, patching the paving and working to keep the corridor open. The engineers had one other vital role in the battle.

Communications was yet to become a specialized function and was then the responsibility of the engineers. To understand the tactics of the war demands recognition of the paucity of the communications. Headquarters were reliant on reports carried tenuously by carrier pigeon, runners, dispatch-riders on horse and motor cycle, or by semaphore, signal lamps or telephone. While line was the quickest and most effective it was also vulnerable to shell fire or accidental cutting. This demanded laborious burying of cables, and the duplication of lines against the probability of their being cut. Although by 1918 several forms of radio were available they were either too heavy and cumbersome or their range was too limited to be effective for use in the attack.

The lack of reliable communications meant that the corps and divisional commanders lost control once the infantry crossed the start-line. Suddenly they had no ability to influence the course of the battle. All they could hope for was occasional reports telling them how far the troops had progressed. This led to the need for rigid and detailed plans based on assumptions of what could hopefully be achieved. It also explains the precisely timed fire plans for the creeping barrages. Something as critical to the success of the battle as the barrage could not be left to the vagaries of the communications and had to be detailed exactly in advance. Once battle was joined the commander lost the flexibility to alter or adapt his plan. This lack of direct and immediate control by the commanders made the battles of WW1 very different from what we have become accustomed from WW2 and more recent conflict. The failure to recognize the impact that the lack of communications had on command and control has resulted in much ill-informed criticism of the commanders. They did their best under the circumstances, of which the plans for the barrages is a good example.

Stan Watson, an engineer, had arrived at Gallipoli on 25 April as a lieutenant. There he built the first pier that famously bore his name. As a captain he supervised the evacuation and was among the last to leave Anzac Cove. At Amiens, now a major, he was in charge of communications for the Australian Corps. As the attack progressed he had a mass of cables run along the verge of the Roman Road, then buried for their protection and laterals laid to each flank. It enabled far better communications for Monash than was customary and he lavished praise (and a DSO) on Watson. After the war Watson returned to his civilian occupation as an engineer with the SA Railways.

***

The battlecraft had been proven. At last all the techniques developed over the previous three years had been integrated. All the cogs of the great wheel of battle were at last meshed. It had been a long gestation but eventually the combined-arms battle had been born. And the Australian Corps had played a role in its birth. Yet the prominence of the Australians and Canadians in the victory only added to the displeasure of those senior British officers who declined to recognize the colonials as soldiers. Their antipathy was so great some preferred to ignore the battle rather than to give credit to those they despised. Although those of the 'dog-in the-manger' attitude were only a minority, their negativity impacted on the historical record and it is only recently that the significance of Amiens is gaining recognition.

It is curious why such an attitude prevailed, particularly when Amiens was a totally joint operation in which the Dominion infantry played their part along with the British tanks, guns, aircraft and logistics, and with all under British command. It could have been hailed as the great 'Empire victory' but the antipathy was so deeply ingrained in some that they preferred the battle to be ignored.

CHAPTER 6

The Battle of Amiens II

'Stabbed in the Back'

Tactics & Strategy

'I am the enemy you killed, my friend.
I knew you in this dark: for so you frowned
Yesterday through me as you jabbed and killed.
I parried: but my hands were loath and cold.
Let us sleep now …

Wilfred Owen[61]

Hamel had shown the cohesion of the Australian Corps. There it had displayed its leadership, discipline and aggression but, most importantly, its grasp of the new tactic of the combined-arms battle that could change the face of battle. This had been recognized by Foch and Haig who had seen the potential for it to break the stalemate and they unleashed it at Amiens, using the same methods on a vaster scale. Since the Franco-Prussian War Europe had stood more or less in awe of German tactical skill but now at last, at Amiens, after nearly four years of war, the tables would be turned and the German Army would lurch into retreat. And it would be a retreat that gained speed as the Hundred Days passed and it was pushed back towards its border.

Strangely there has been a reluctance to recognize the victory of the BEF over the German Army. It is hard to conceive that this is due solely to British modesty. Something, however, arose to subvert the triumph. The victory of the BEF on the Western Front in 1918 was the clinching event of the war but that is not how it is portrayed or remembered. We have allowed the legends to distort our perception of how the war concluded.

Wars end because one side loses, which may be for a number of reasons. The enemy may have greater numbers, better strategy or tactics, better weapons, leadership or morale; public support may collapse; or the economy fail. Many may be the reasons but loss means humiliation and the greatest humiliation is where it is due to the defeat of the nation's armed forces. Amiens was the tipping point for the German army. In the period from 8 August till 11 November the allies drove the Germans back from successive defensive lines to its frontier and mauled it until it was no longer capable of resistance. The German army faced catastrophic defeat and the great humiliation.

For the German army this was a very bitter pill. Its vaunted general staff and professional soldiers had been defeated by those they had regarded as 'amateurs', and by what the Kaiser had derided as 'a contemptible little army'. For the pride of the army, its prestige, and their plans for its recovery, it was better to deny defeat. There were many causes to which they could point to excuse Germany's loss other than defeat on the battlefield: there was the blockade that cut off the flow of strategic supplies, and also starved the population; the failure to fully adapt its industry to war production; the inability of the submarine campaign to isolate Britain; the eventual collapse of its allies; and, towards late 1918, growing political anarchy within Germany itself. This, the latter, was chosen by the General Staff as their scapegoat and blame was laid on 'the November criminals' of the Catholic Centre, the Social Democrats and the Jews.[62] It was, they claimed, that cartel which had inflicted 'the Stab-in-the-Back', *dolchstoss*, on the German army. Were it not, they alleged, for the November criminals the army would have continued the struggle.

This boast, though, defies the reality: by early October the Hindenburg Line, the last established defences, had been over-run; the allies were advancing rapidly to the German frontier. Although there remained a million German soldiers on the Western Front, few were now fighting; and there were no reserves left to plug the gaps. The German army was defeated but, rather than admit their humiliation, its leaders desperately sought excuses and 'someone to blame'. This they found in the *dolchstosslegende*.[63]

***

By September, recognising the probability of defeat, the German government began seeking a means to end the war at least cost. Anticipating the vengeance of the French and British they turned to the Americans and to President Woodrow Wilson's Fourteen Points, an outline formula for an armistice rather than surrender. It avoided apportioning blame or making demands for reparations. On those terms they sought to open negotiations with the Americans who quickly passed the responsibility to the French and British who understandably refused to accept the constraints of the Fourteen Points. In mid-October Wilson informed the Germans that his Fourteen Points could not form the basis for an armistice. Yet, despite the warning, when the delegates met on 11 November in the railway carriage in the Compiègne Forest the Germans affected surprise when rigid terms, essentially of surrender, were laid down. Yet with their army in disarray and civil war looming they had no option than to concede. These conditions were subsequently formalized in the Treaty of Versailles which included loss of territory, heavy reparations and severe limits on the size and structure of its army and navy. The wisdom of the harshness of the terms is conjectural and there is little doubt they provided the grievances that fuelled the next conflict. The immediate consequence was to provide Germany with two excuses which it used to mitigate the pain of its surrender.

Firstly, they claimed, Germany had been tricked into surrender. They had begun discussions in the belief it was based of the Fourteen Points that would lead to a negotiated settlement but had then been forced to accept surrender terms. They claimed that in expectation of a negotiated armistice they had begun demobilizing their army and by the time they found they were to be given no option than surrender it was too late to halt the process. They had, they claimed, been tricked. This legend laid blame on the allies. The second excuse blamed the German people, elements of whom they claimed had failed the army and 'stabbed it in the back'. How, they asked, could their valiant soldiers continue their defence of the fatherland while behind them the nation was collapsing into civil war and anarchy, betrayed by the Jews, Catholics and socialists?

The fabrication was accepted at face value, not only by the German people, but eventually by many who had fought against them. *Dolchstoss* was a calculated lie, designed deliberately to obscure the truth of the German army's defeat. This is now well established, initially by the German scholar Wilhelm Deist, but it is still refuted by some. It is the most pernicious of the legends and its consequences the most damaging.[64]

***

By denying its military defeat the German army avoided humiliation. So with its dignity intact it set about rebuilding, helped by having retained the best of the old army in the rump allowed by the Treaty. While the allies wallowed in the complacency of victory the Germans clinically analysed the reasons for their defeat and devised the tactic for future success – *blitzkrieg*. The pride of the German army was, however, fragile and needed guarding from too close scrutiny. This the Nazi Party offered, and by protecting the army it came soon to control it.

Craftily, the legend was also used to sow disunity among the allies. The heavy reparations, demanded under the terms of the Treaty, were blamed on a French lust for revenge. This led some in Britain to accept the view of Germany having been tricked, and their sympathy swung to the Germans. And, *ipso facto*, if tricked, they had not been defeated on the Western Front. As the years passed the memory of Amiens and the Hundred Days faded. The legend of *dolchstoss* denied the allies their victory and hence their collective triumph. It became easier to sympathize with the horror than to argue for the triumph.

***

With the doubts sown by *dolchstoss,* other theories of the course of the war that detracted from victory on the Western Front gained credence. David Lloyd George, prime minister from 1916, had a famously poor relationship with the army leadership. The passionate Welshman had great difficulty communicating with Haig, the dour, inarticulate Scot, or his principal military advisor, the aloof General Sir William Robertson, Chief of the General Staff. Lloyd George abhorred the slaughter on the Western Front and had advocated flanking alternatives in Salonika, the Balkans, or Italy, which the generals regarded as both a distraction from the primary focus and also as political interference. The animosity ran so deeply that Lloyd George was loath to give the generals credit for their victory and subscribed to the war being 'drawn'. Then, probably with malice at heart, he identified a junior general and an Australian to boot, General Monash, over his own, as the greatest general of the war.[65] This was a condemnation of British army leadership that cut to the quick of British pride in its military achievement. It was also a denial to the public of their collective triumph which can be linked to the switch in British public opinion in the late 1920s from earlier support to condemnation of the war.

Lloyd George's reluctance to credit his generals with the defeat of the German army was readily embraced by others with equivalent agendas. Those with loyalties to the Royal Navy, the traditional defender of the realm, were reluctant to see the credit for victory going to the army. Surely, they claimed, it was the blockade or the anti-submarine campaign that had been the war-winner – the Western Front was merely a wasteful side-show.[66] Also the horror of the Western front had spawned new concepts of warfare through which it was hoped in future to avoid a recurrence of the slaughter. In the 1920s the Italian aviator Giulio Douhet conceived ideas of 'total war' with the use of strategic bombing to shatter civilian morale.[67] Air power would make the battlefield irrelevant. Likewise, Basil Liddell Hart, the British military theorist, formulated his concept of the 'Indirect Approach' of striking at the enemy's point of weakness, rather than facing the full weight of his military strength on the battlefield.[68] These theories were held up as evidence that the efforts of the BEF had been unnecessary. Why had they suffered the slaughter when other options may have been available? Increasingly the carnage of the

Western Front was decried as having been pointless. The public had taken ownership of the war and was imposing its own imagining.

***

There the perspective lay for the next thirty years. WW2 saw the evolution of a more agile form of war that by contrast re-enforced the ghastliness of WW1. Then curiously in Britain the decade from the mid-1950s became an incubator of legends of WW1. Several factors, political and social, combined to refocus British public interest on the Great War. The Suez crisis, the Cuban Missile crisis and Vietnam showed that peace was tenuous and fragile. War could now mean nuclear conflict and this fear spawned pacifist movements and 'ban the bomb' marches. At this time most of the books exemplifying the horror of the battles of 1916 and 17 were published. The British public was also coming to terms with the end of imperial power and economic stagnation. There was a search for someone to blame and conveniently a cause of British woes could be sheeted home to WW1. The Edwardians and their generals became the butt of ridicule and satire. WW1 became a whipping boy,[69] justified by *Oh What a Lovely War* and *Blackadder*.

***

At last, however, there is a growing recognition that at Amiens and in the battles of the Hundred Days the British Army and its dominion contingents had their finest hour. Amiens is now being recognized as the decisive battle of WW1, that which set the scene for Germany's defeat. Ludendorff recognized its significance and called it *der schwarze Tag*, 'the black day of the German army in the Great War'. Amiens and the Hundred Days saw the German army driven back towards its borders in increasing disorder and saved only by the Armistice. Few battles in the next war were as strategically decisive as Amiens had been, possibly only those fought by the US Navy at Midway and the USSR at Stalingrad.

Its victory at Amiens should have been regarded by Britain on a par with Waterloo as a uniquely British battle of decisive strategic importance, yet for nearly a century it has been ignored. Many books have been written on the battles in Flanders and the Somme, yet only one has been written exclusively on the greatest battle of them all.[70] A number of reasons have been suggested as to why it was overlooked. In part it was because of the brilliance of its success. Casualties to the BEF were so minimal on 8 August that in WW1 terms it did not seem to register as a significant battle. The BEF suffered less than 6,000 casualties on 8 August, a figure that suggested it was a minor engagement. That this paucity of casualties was the consequence of a dramatic change to the approach to battle failed to register.

The combination of tactical success with relatively few casualties signalled a tidal shift in the course of the war. Amiens confirmed a new tactical approach to battle and, if its success could be matched with an appropriate strategy, it could be a war-winning combination. But why had it taken four years of war to devise the necessary tactics? And could a complementary strategy be developed?

***

Tactics. What accounts for the allied victory of 1918? How could the BEF transform from an army that in April had faced defeat under the weight of the German Spring Offensive to one that achieved victory in November? It was a remarkable change of fortune that astounded not only Germany but the allies themselves. By mid-1918, after the German Spring offensive had been blocked, it became clear that with the flood of US forces into France an allied victory was assured, although it was believed this could not happen until late 1919 when the Americans had learned the skills of soldiering. Amiens and the Hundred Days upset the calculations and brought forward the chance for victory, far earlier than had been anticipated. How had this transformation occurred?

At Amiens the BEF found the key to victory, and it lay in the unification of its battlecraft, tactical and strategic skills. We have seen the evolution that occurred in battlecraft, the steady enhancement of the fighting skills, techniques and weaponry of the infantry, artillery and tanks over the preceding few years. These were then integrated into the tactical concept of the combined-arms battle. The missing element was a matching strategy and this was to come from Amiens. This transformation of the battlecraft, tactics and strategy was dynamic. For a century, until 1914, attack had been the dominant phase of war and battles had been fought in a prescribed manner, almost to a ritual. The respective capabilities of the infantry, artillery and cavalry were employed but not in unison. At Waterloo, Gettysburg and Sedan the artillery had battered the infantry, the cavalry had charged, and then the infantry had attacked. Each fought in succession and generally in the absence of any direct support from the other arms. And it was through attack that the battles were won. But the nature of war had changed over the course of the century. The wealth and organization of the nation-state now allowed for vast conscript armies; bureaucracy and the new telegraph enabled rapid mobilization; and railways could deploy troops speedily to the frontiers. There, however, the system stalled, for the recent innovations in defence frustrated the offensive: barbed wire, concrete and the machine-gun stopped the attack. By 1915 defence had become the dominant phase of war.

The Germans had attained a mastery of defence. The grand plan for the conquest of France, prepared by the German Chief of Staff, Count Alfred von Schlieffen in 1905, called for an offensive by the bulk of the German army, deployed in the north, to strike through Belgium and encircle Paris. An essential ingredient of the plan relied on the remaining German forces to effectively block the inevitable French counter-offensive in the south. An outnumbered German force had to be able to withstand a concentrated French attack. Emphasis was given by Schlieffen to the study and development of the techniques of defence. Consequently, although in 1914 the attack to encircle Paris failed, the defending southern flank still held firm. Throughout the war the Germans refined their tactical skills of defence. They developed the concept of defence in depth, with a series of lines of trenches over a distance of up to five kilometres using the protection of reverse slopes, together with camouflage and concealment. A subsequent refinement was to forsake the trenches for a checker-board of strong points, sited for all-round defence with each providing mutual support to its neighbour. These strongpoints would be shielded by obstacles to deflect the attack into killing grounds with the intent not to repel, but to absorb and destroy. Plans for both quick and deliberate counter-attack were an integral part of the tactic. The German army had transformed defence from a passive to a highly active and lethal phase of war. It was so effective that for four years the allies found German defences difficult and very costly to breach. But now it was to come apart in the face of the combined-arms attack.

By the end of August in 1914, although the Schlieffen Plan had failed the Germans had been able to seize much of Belgium and large areas of eastern France before the Allies could consolidate the front. They were then largely content to sit in their defences and let the Allies expend their manpower in costly attacks – the war of attrition. Yet the Allies had no option than to attack if they were to recover the ground lost in 1914 before entering negotiations. When at Verdun in 1916 the Germans swung to the offensive, their heavy losses proved to them the futility of attack without a battle-winning tactic. Thereafter on the Western Front they remained largely on the defensive until they believed they had the formula for victory in the shock tactics of the Spring Offensive. That tactic broke down, however, when through its very success the shock troops, racing ahead, outstripped the range of their supporting artillery.

For the attack to be effective on the WW1 battlefield required an integrated approach. It was quickly apparent that machine-guns left the cavalry irrelevant, and it was relegated to awaiting the breakout following a successful battle. Its place was taken by the tank but they were slow and cumbersome and, while effective against machine-guns, they were vulnerable to artillery. The infantry were vulnerable to both machine-guns and artillery and their attack was slowed by barbed-wire. The guns however could cut the wire and neutralize the machine-guns, while the tanks could crush both wire and machine-guns. Realisation dawned that success could be achieved by all the arms working closely together to provide mutual support and protection – the combined-arms tactic was born.

From its formation the BEF was a developing and evolving force. It had grown rapidly in size since 1914. The combined-arms battle of 1918 was very different in character to those of the earlier years of the war. It was the product of the techniques that evolved over the course of the war. Each of the major battles from 1915 had seen a desperate search for a battle-winning idea. Steadily the new concepts were floated, tested and either proven or discarded. By late 1917 most of the separate elements of the combined-arms battle had been identified. It was not until 1918 that the various techniques were linked together into a tactical plan.

Taking and holding ground was the key objective of the WW1 battle. This was the task of the infantry: the other arms were there to help the infantry achieve their objective. Yet to integrate their actions as demanded by the combined-arms tactic requires a high degree of skill, confidence and experience across all the arms involved. To develop the techniques required seasoned and battle-hardened formations which were in short supply in the

BEF in 1918 but could be found in the Dominion contingents. Since 1914 the number of British divisions had grown ten-fold through first regular, then volunteer, and by 1918 conscript numbers. The dominions had seen equivalent early growth but then declining numbers of volunteers. In consequence, where British expertise had been dissipated across an enlarging force, that of the dominions was concentrated in a contracting force. Consequently it was the Canadian and Australian Corps and the New Zealand Division with only a handful of British divisions, which led the way in developing the techniques of the combined-arms battle. While the logic of the concept was obvious to most commanders in the BEF it was nigh impossible for it to be trialled, developed and introduced by the inexperienced conscripts that comprised most British divisions by 1918. This meant the Australian Corps played a major part in developing and refining the combined-arms tactics. Its contribution to the success of the Hundred Days was significant.

It was through the combined-arms tactic that the allies, primarily the BEF, won their battles in 1918 that led to victory. It was at Amiens that the component elements of the combined-arms battle came together. Amiens was the opening movement to the crescendo of the war. Here at last all the players in the military orchestra came together to work in harmony. The generals could at last, as Monash described it, 'orchestrate the battle'.[71] No longer did the tactical instruments play solo but the guns, the infantry, the tanks and the planes were now unified in a symphony of violence, each complementing and harmonizing with the other.

***

Understandably this change was not recognized by the public. The photographs showed soldiers in the same uniforms, carrying the same rifles, wearing the same helmets, peering out of the same trenches, or stumbling across the same shell-shattered landscape. The casualty lists in the papers were as long and as tragic as ever. The public believed the battles were being fought as they had been since 1914. They had difficulty seeing the changes evolving over the years. Then when the tide turned they asked why had it taken four years to achieve? They failed to recognize that a completely new way of waging war had to be developed. A hundred years of established tactical methods had to be discarded and new techniques identified and tested, introduced and then integrated. That it was done so quickly, and so effectively, was a remarkable achievement that the public failed to recognise.

Strangely, it is only over the past forty years that historians have come to the realization that it was the major changes in the way the battles were fought that led to victory over Germany. Despite the sudden transformation of the fortunes of the allies, where tactical success over the Germans suddenly became commonplace from July 1918, neither the reason nor the effect were actively investigated. When recognition dawned in the early 1980s of the change in tactics its cause was dubbed 'the Learning Curve' by Peter Simkins, a leading British military historian, and this modest descriptive has stuck.[72] It may account in part for the public's failure to credit the BEF with its great victory at Amiens and in the Hundred Days. The soldiers knew what they had achieved but, as it was difficult to describe, the public remained in ignorance.

Dolchstoss played a large part in the failure to recognize the change in the tactics. The claim that German defeat lay in the stab-in-the-back from the 'November criminals', rather than a transformation of military tactics, appeared to have logic and was simpler for the public to believe. It was only Wilhelm Deist's revelations in the 1970s of the fabrication of the legend that gave impetus to the search for the real reason for German defeat. The war-shattering importance of the combined-arms tactic had been overlooked and with it the major part played in its development by the AIF. Even now few Australians realise this role the Diggers played in the defeat of the German Army.

***

Military Strategy. While tactics are the techniques used to win battles, strategy is the art of winning wars. Strategy is usually considered in terms of national strategy, its overarching objectives, or as military strategy, defeating the armed force of the enemy. While the tactics applied on 8 August had been brilliantly successful, could they be matched by the strategy?

Haig and Foch, seeing tactical success, grasped at the straw of the long-dreamed classic breakout, with the cavalry pouring through into the German rear to achieve the strategic objective of a battle of annihilation. That was the military strategy with which they had persisted from 1914, and which they still demanded for 9 August. The battle of Amiens, however, was over.

What the Fourth Army had set out to do had been done. The tactics had succeeded; the strategy could not. The troops were exhausted and there remained only 147 of the 530 tanks that had deployed at the start of the day. All the ingredients and the complex and elaborate planning for a renewal of a successful combined-arms battle were missing. Targets had to be identified, the guns repositioned and registered, and ammunition had to be stockpiled. Most seriously, the Germans had once more consolidated their front. Late that day and over the night of 8/9 August ten German divisions had been rushed forward to confront the five forward Australian and Canadian divisions. If there ever had been 'a window of opportunity' it was now firmly closed. Yet, in response to orders, the staffs of Fourth Army and the two corps set about planning the breakout battle. But it was ad hoc; little could be cobbled together in one night, and there was neither the time nor the resources for a combined-arms battle.

Throughout the war the tactics and the strategy had been intertwined. Until 1918 the German tactics of defence in depth had frustrated the attack and any chance of strategic breakout. Now with the combined-arms tactic the attackers could at last break in, overwhelm the defence and break through into the rear, but there the battle stalled. The capacity to encircle and exploit had been lost. That had been the role of the fast-moving cavalry, unleashed into the enemy's rear areas to deny him the chance to rally. But the machine-gun stopped the cavalry and trains quickly deployed the reserves to plug the gap opened by the break-through. The strategic concept of the annihilation battle was a lost cause. The Germans had seen this early in the war and had disbanded their cavalry divisions: Haig clung to his in hope. It was the Germans who, although having largely ignored the tank in the war, then recognized its potential that saw the panzers rampaging through France in 1940. But that was another war and on 9 August Rawlinson needed a solution to his immediate problem.

***

Over the next three days the two corps launched a succession of ill-planned, uncoordinated and under-resourced attacks and, as was customary, casualties quickly mounted, for little success. Finally, Lieutenant-General Sir Arthur Currie, the Canadian commander, stood up to Rawlinson and demanded an end to it. Rawlinson concurred and took the issue to Haig, who in turn confronted Foch who reluctantly conceded. Then Haig, inspired by what had been achieved, ordered a similar combined-arms attack with limited objectives by Third Army to the north that also met with success. As early as 1915 Rawlinson had advocated a strategy of 'bite and hold', based on a concept of well-resourced attacks but with limited objectives, rather than grandiose dreams of breakout.[73] Yet for three years the commanders had persisted in that dream. German defence frustrated each offensive but they continued to be pushed mercilessly and as each offensive faded away into eventual stalemate they had to settle for the consolation of their small gains. They were essentially fighting a strategy of bite and hold but refused to accept its reality: better always to dream of unleashing the cavalry to achieve the great battle of annihilation. With Amiens realization of reality finally dawned and Rawlinson's concept at last gained acceptance. Amiens had proved the brilliance of the combined-arms tactic, now belatedly it forced acceptance of the bite and hold strategy.

The Germans confronted a succession of intense, surprise attacks, but with limited objectives, along their front. Lost was their capacity to move reserves in anticipation to the vicinity of the next well-advertised battle even before it was launched. With the exception of Verdun and the Spring Offensive the Germans on the Western Front had relied mainly on their mastery of defence to erode the allied strength. Suddenly the combined-arms attack could sweep away their defences, while the surprise that could now accompany the bite and hold strategy meant their reserves arrived too late to influence the battle. They struggled to react to the multitude of attacks and the key elements of their defensive strategy came apart. Success of the combined-arms battle had shown Foch and Haig the means to win on the battlefield and now acceptance of the bite and hold strategy provided the formula to win the war.

***

National Strategy. In war the national will to achieve victory is vital: armies cannot persist if the nation does not support their effort. There lies the rationale of the *dolchstosslegende*; the German people were no longer supporting their army. In contrast British commitment remained steadfast. While in August

1914 the British Empire was not attuned to war, within a few years it had re-geared itself to war with the resources of the dominions flowing to the factories of Britain and then for distribution to the British forces fighting in campaigns from East Africa, Mesopotamia, Salonika and Palestine to the Western Front. The resources of the Empire had been mobilized and its effect is seen at its greatest on the Western Front. The success of the new tactic and the new military strategy relied on those behind the front line to produce the materiel—the weapons, the ammunition, the food, the clothing, the medical stores and all the paraphernalia needed to sustain a vast army in battle—and then to move it where, and when, it was needed. These two elements, war production and logistics, were crucial to victory. Logistics became a linkage between the military and the national strategies.

By 1917 the BEF in France had grown to a strength of two million. To sustain it required 200,000 tons of stores each week, to be shipped across the Channel, transported to the Front and then distributed. Once landed the transportation was primarily by rail which meant the totally inadequate French network had to be restructured and expanded. Five-hundred additional British railway engines were brought across the Channel and several thousand kilometres of new railway line were laid. Amiens was the lynch-pin of the Southern line of communications through which passed half the total tonnage and its importance as a logistics nodal point had been a major factor in the decision of Foch and Haig leading to the battle of 8 August.[74]

Once at the rail-head the stores had to be moved forward. Early in the war this had been by horse and cart but this means gave way increasingly to motor transport as thousands of lorries flowed off the British production lines. By the end of the war the BEF had 50,000 lorries in use while the German Army remained essentially horse-drawn. The BEF had fashioned a vast and comprehensive logistics system that could meet the needs of the combined-arms battle and then sustain the force, once it broke out of static warfare into the advance of the Hundred Days.

***

With logistics and the combined-arms battle mutually dependent, so too were both reliant on war production. Without the shells for the guns there could be neither barrage nor counter-battery fire. Without well-made and reliable shells the creeping barrage would lose its effectiveness and the counter-battery fire would fail. Much depended on what happened hundreds of miles from the battlefield.

Britain's industry had to adapt to the war. The scandal of the 'shell crisis' of May 1915, in which failure in production limited each gun to firing only four shells per day, led to the fall of the Asquith government and the appointment of Lloyd George as Minister of Munitions. The production rate rose rapidly from approximately 80,000 shells per month to over four million, largely through the labour of a million women who had been brought into the ammunition factories. Hand in hand with the massive increase in production was an equally crucial improvement in the quality of those shells. It had been judged in 1915 that due to faulty fuzes only 50% of the shells detonated, while the infamous 'drop-shorts' often resulted from badly measured charges. Rectifying such problems was essential to an effective barrage on which the combined-arms tactic relied. From what had been a minimal war industry base in 1914 Britain and the Empire had built a massive capability by 1918.

By 1917 Britain's war production had exceeded that of Germany in all sectors: tanks, aircraft, munitions and guns.[75] Germany was defeated on the factory floor as well as on the battlefield. Support of the combined-arms battle was not simply an issue of defence production. Behind success on the battlefield, and in the factory, lay commitment across a wide range of skills and disciplines. The war unleashed a torrent of innovation. New ideas were brought quickly to effective use: tanks and sound-ranging, sonar and depth charges, light machine-guns, gas masks and anti-tank mines were conceived, designed and put to production. Existing systems were revised, improved and refined. Despite the negatives of death and destruction the war also generated great creative energy.

In significant part the victory at Amiens was due to the effort behind the front. The battle could not have been fought or won without the improvements that had occurred in the logistics and production. Now these elements of national strategy were meshing with the new combined-arms tactics. And at last, as a consequence of the battle, a relevant and attainable military strategy had been recognized. All the components for victory were in hand and all that was left for Germany was dwindling time before inevitable military defeat.

CHAPTER 7

The Battle of Mont St Quentin

'Lions Led by Donkeys'

Leadership

Pay well, command well, hang well.
　　　Injunction on leadership by
　　　English Civil War general,
　　　　　Sir Ralph Hopgood

I have returned to these:
The farm, and the kindly bush, and the young calves lowing:
But all that my mind sees
Is a quaking bog in a mist – stark, snapped trees,
And the dark Somme flowing.
　　　　　　　Vance Palmer

Following the success of 8 August the battle quickly regressed to standards reminiscent of 1916–17. The Australians and Canadians battered at Lihons which, after heavy casualties, fell on 11 August to what had been poorly co-ordinated and supported attacks. It was a relief when on 14 August Haig switched the offensive northward to the Third Army front. For a week the Australian Corps licked its wounds while the Canadians moved north to rejoin the First Army. On 21 August the Germans began to fall back slowly to a defensive line that ran through Peronne, Bapaume and Arras. Here they planned to consolidate and to spend the winter.

The Australian Corps followed, deployed astride the Somme with the 3rd Division on the north bank and the 1st on the south. With Haig's focus now on the battle in the north, the Fourth Army was directed to limit its pressure to sufficient only to retain on its front those German reserves which the Battle of Amiens had attracted. This did not satisfy the eager, thrusting Monash who employed an active pursuit that he termed 'patrol activity', a ruse that drew a 'blind eye' from Rawlinson. In a succession of vicious little battles the Corps advanced quickly, with the 2nd and 5th Divisions replacing the 1st on the south bank of the Somme on 26 August. The Australians closed on the Somme bend, a place where the westward flowing river, which the Australians had been following upstream, hooks sharply to the south. Here at the bend the river is wide and shallow with a maze of marshes and channels lying in front of the old walled town of Peronne on the far bank near the point of the bend.

The 2nd and the 5th Divisions cleared the German defences from the bank opposite Peronne on 29 August but then Monash changed his plan of taking Peronne by frontal assault across the Somme.[76] He recognized that the hill feature of Mont St Quentin, less than two kilometres north of Peronne, was the vital ground, and whoever held the hill, controlled the town. Although less than one hundred metres high the Mont, with its bare and gentle slope, dominates the surrounding area. A frontal assault river-crossing through the swamps to take Peronne while under observation from Mont St Quentin, would have been very costly. Consequently he had the 3rd Division continue to push east on the northern bank to secure the ground north of the Somme bend, while the engineers bridged the river behind them. The 2nd Division would then cross the Somme and attack the Mont directly from the west.

This was an audacious plan. Monash was changing the centre of gravity of his force to the left flank. It was to be achieved by the complex and vulnerable manoeuvre of moving the 2nd Division laterally across the front, over the Somme, through the 3rd Division, and then to attack Mont St Quentin. On 30 August the weary battalions of the 3rd Division, some of whom had been moving and fighting for eighty hours without break, managed to clear the bridging site, and to secure the assembly area for the 2nd Division, which then moved by night into position for a dawn attack on the morning of 31 August. There was no time even for 'the ritual' of the pre-attack hot meal: all that could be got to the Diggers in time was a tot of rum.

***

With the completion of this deployment Monash's contribution to the battle was largely complete. He had placed his force in position from where it could now attack the enemy with the greatest chance of success. There was little more he could now do that would influence the outcome. Lack of communications largely took the battle out of his hands. From this time on, success or failure lay with the junior leaders and the Diggers. That they were now favourably positioned after such complex deployment had been made possible by the skill of the staff and the endurance of the Diggers.

Since March the tempo of battle had changed. After nearly four years of almost static warfare the German Spring Offensive had suddenly imposed the fluidity of withdrawal on the BEF. Then with Amiens, and the start of the offensive, they faced a new challenge to which they had to adapt. The pursuit was a phase of war to which the BEF was unaccustomed and which demanded different skills. To maintain the momentum they had to deny the Germans the chance to settle and consolidate their defence: speed, albeit that of the foot-soldier, was essential to bounce the enemy from his hasty defences. There was no time for laborious step-by-step preparation for the attack that had been customary in the past.

Now all procedures for the attack had to be in concert and a number of activities performed in unison. This is a system the army knows as battle procedure: 'the concurrent processes by which reconnaissance, planning, orders and preliminary movement is completed and troops deployed'.[77] At the first sign of an imminent attack a 'warning order' is distributed giving the objective and key timings. Then, while the commander makes his reconnaissance and prepares his plan, the troops can continue their preparations or begin to move, while subordinate commanders gather to receive their orders. They in turn complete their reconnaissance, prepare and give their orders while deployment continues, meals are eaten or rest taken.

At Gallipoli battle procedure had been rudimentary, and it was rarely used in the set-piece battles before 1918, but it had been quickly relearned after Amiens and was becoming a polished procedure in the Australian Corps. That Monash could manoeuvre his force with such speed and deploy it with velocity was a reflection of the competence of the staff and the skill of the commanders. Having mastered the complexity of the combined-arms battle and adapted so quickly to open warfare and the intricacies of the advance, suggests leaders of great competence, yet the public labels them as 'donkeys' and many continue to see them from such a perspective.

***

The shibboleth 'Lions led by donkeys' (or asses or mules) has been often used. It has described British commanders in the Crimean War, French leaders in the Franco-Prussian War, the Russian contingent in the Boxer Rebellion and both British and German leadership in WW1. Its use as a title of a book by Alan Clark, highly critical of British WW1 generals,[78] re-introduced it to the British public in the 1960s. In concert with the musical *Oh What a Lovely War* and, in the 1980s, the *Blackadder* TV series, it reflected the popular perception of that time. Yet it has been suggested it said more about contemporary British attitudes than British command in WW1. It is now considered a view that has been in large part discredited by research.[79] It remains however, the perception of many Australians.

There is a widely held belief that Australian lives were casually sacrificed by British command. This perception is re-enforced by the populist and mildly xenophobic 'aussie-aussie-aussie' sub-culture reflected in the film *Gallipoli* and much of the centenary commentary. There also remains a strong antipathy towards British leaders who are seen as responsible for the high Australian casualties. Generally, however, the growing interest in the study of the war is leading to a more reasoned analysis.

Surprisingly, Australian condemnation of leadership is directed exclusively at British leaders, while Australians are excused, as too are those British officers who were seconded in command of Australian formations.

The Assault on Mont St Quentin, 31 August 1918

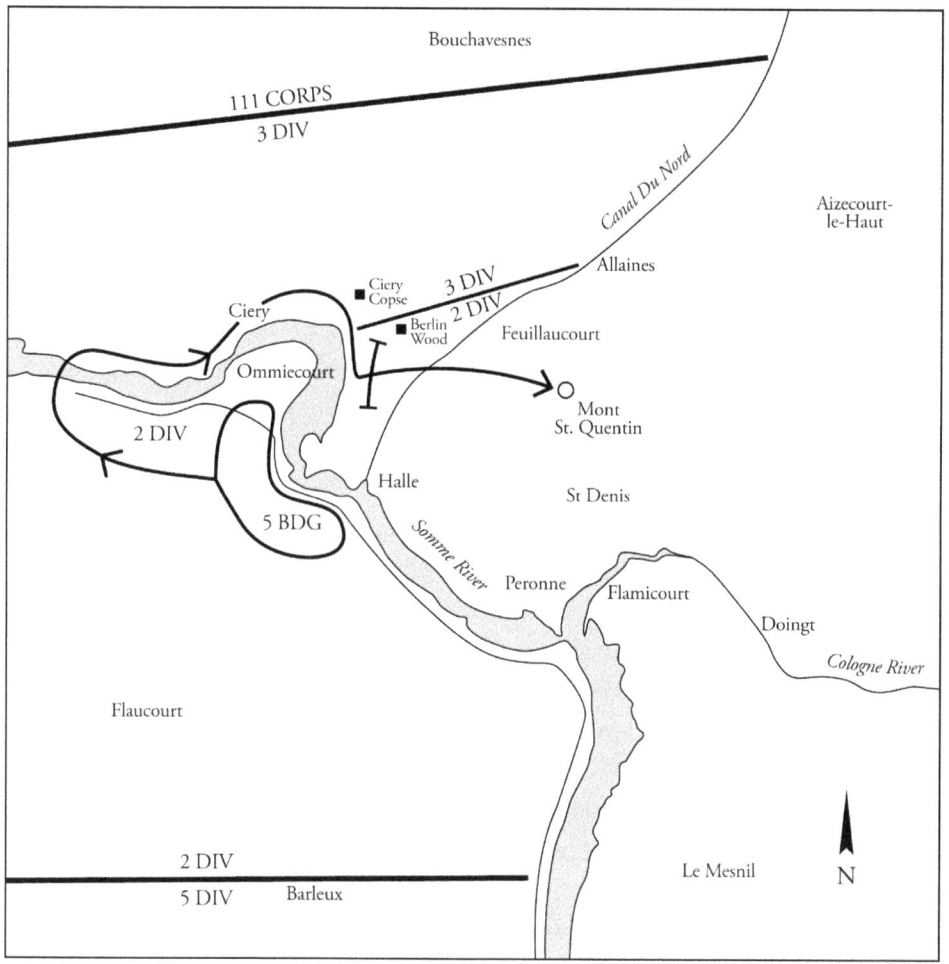

Although Australian leaders at all levels had also to constantly gamble with the lives of their men and made errors as serious as their British counterparts they remain immune from criticism. The Australian proclivity to 'lop the tall poppy' seems to be confined to the British while Australian shortcomings are overlooked. Yet while Monash is revered as a great leader his Canadian counterpart, Lieutenant-General Sir Arthur Currie, faced savage criticism from his troops and countrymen, forcing him after the war to take the issue to court in an effort to clear his name. He was accused of driving his men too hard in the Hundred Days to gain personal credit from the British.[80] This accusation could have been made as easily of Monash; however, our WW1 leaders were spared criticism. What then was expected of the leaders?

Leadership today is the subject of many studies and theories, and there is often a confusing overlap with management theory. The type and style of leadership varies significantly depending on the span and nature of the command and the circumstance of the moment. For a general to motivate 100,000 men for a battle is very different from that needed by a second-lieutenant to get half a dozen scared and exhausted men to assault a machine-gun nest fifty metres to their front. That which was required of Haig and his army commanders was rather more managerial skill than inspirational leadership. The span of their command, and the size of their formations were so vast, and the means of communication so limited, they had little prospect of instilling inspiration. What was required of them was to marshal and co-ordinate the resources available to them, integrate all the disparate elements of their commands into a cohesive and unified force, and produce a plan for battle that was comprehensive but at the same time simple. This was the challenge they faced, and which after several years they mastered.

Recent studies of WW1 have shown that there was a distinct evolution in the methods of command and leadership over its course. Where in the early years the detailed planning of the battles lay at army level, as skill and confidence at the lower levels grew, so responsibility for detail was delegated to the corps and lower. We have seen how the input of the Corps staff and divisional commanders influenced the planning of the Battle of Hamel. Now, at Mont St Quentin, Rawlinson left the conduct of the battle entirely in the hands of Monash who in turn delegated the detail of the battle to his divisional and brigade commanders. With this delegation of responsibility went a change in leadership style. The higher commanders increasingly became managers with leadership becoming the responsibility of lower levels. Haig and his army commanders, and lately the corps commanders, would decide where the battles would be fought, allocate resources, and then let their subordinates get on with the job. Responsibility for leadership was thrust downward.

***

The assault on Mont St Quentin began at 5 am, 'first light', on 31 August. The barrage came down, not a creeping barrage which could not be safely programmed in the time available, but fire from five artillery brigades on the two main defensive lines facing the assault. The German guns retaliated immediately with heavy defensive fire that lasted for hours, but it fell on the far bank of the Somme opposite Peronne. The Germans had been expecting the attack, but not from the direction it came. The first surprise was achieved by the Australians.

The 5th Brigade stormed the hill with two battalions leading (the 17th and 20th). Speed and violence was the essence of the attack and the Diggers went up the hill, often at the run, yelling and cheering and dislodging from the defences far greater numbers of Germans than expected. The second surprise was to the enemy: the defenders far outnumbered the attackers. The hill was held by the best part of two German divisions including the elite 2nd Prussian Guards, while there were elements of five divisions holding the Mont St Quentin-Peronne objective.

The velocity of the assault was decisive and the two assaulting battalions over-ran the German defences and, with few casualties, reached the top of the hill while behind them hundreds of Germans streamed into captivity. Rawlinson was shaving at 8 am when he heard to his delighted astonishment

Men of the 24th Battalion moments before their assault to clear the hill on 1 September.
Source: AWM E03142

that Mont St Quentin had fallen. Celebration, however, was premature. The mass of German numbers was too great and the 5th Brigade was forced back from the crest and consolidated just below the summit. Meanwhile the indefatigable 3rd Division assaulted the feature to the north of the Mont to secure the left flank of the 2nd Division and, on the right, the reserve battalion (the 19th) of the 5th Brigade advanced on Peronne from the north. The time for bold charges had passed: now the battle became a vicious struggle to clear or hold each trench. It was a frantic day of confused and bloody fighting, attack and counter-attack, a close infantry struggle in which survival rated as highly as victory. But by the end of the day the ground taken in the morning was all in Australian hands. A wedge had been hammered into the German defences and the scene was set for an Australian triumph. The leadership of the junior officers and NCOs had been decisive.

***

Success in the battle had devolved quickly from the management of the higher command to the leadership of the junior officers and NCOs. Victory hinged on the corporals, sergeants and lieutenants leading their sections and platoons, and where those men fell, in soldiers stepping up to complete the job. There lay the remarkable resilience of the AIF. Essentially leadership is getting people to willingly do what the leader wants them to do. When this entails also putting their lives at risk then a new dimension is introduced. The Australian Corps of 1918 was a highly homogeneous force. Its junior leaders had grown from its ranks. The officers and NCOs were originally soldiers from within the battalions in which they now led. The men knew them and respected them. They had reached their rank by their competence as leaders. But this competence was not one they were taught but which they acquired. Formal leadership training is a recent phenomenon. The aspiring lieutenant of WW1 probably received a leadership lecture in which he heard that to be a good leader he needed qualities such as courage, bravery and determination, although they were not necessarily qualities that would differentiate him from a good follower.

It would have only been by example and instinct that he would have acquired the techniques that are now titled 'functional' leadership. Intuitively he would have realised his primary focus had to be in getting the job

Haig with, on his left, Rawlinson and on his right Plumer. Source: AWM H12241

done: getting the men to follow him in 'jumping the bags', or holding off the attacking enemy. So his first responsibility was to achieve the mission. Winning will always be the primary objective of a leader in any army. But to do this he has to weld the men together as a team. The greater their confidence in him and in their mates, the better they would fight. So team cohesion becomes the second focus. Then thirdly is consideration of the individuals who comprise the team. This was guided by the old adage that 'a chain is as strong as its weakest link'. The leader must get to know the men who make up his team. Each has to feel he belongs and has a role to play, and hopefully sees it as an important role. To achieve this the leader has to know each man individually; his personality, his capabilities and his needs. Although the concept of functional leadership was not formalized until the 1960s it is apparent its principles were being applied instinctively in the AIF. For such tired men to keep flogging themselves forward and then driving themselves into their attacks shows both high morale and sound leadership. WW2 research showed that a soldier fights more *for* someone (his team), rather than *against* somebody (poor old Fritz). The same study shows that the single most important factor that sustains a man in combat is the support he receives from his immediate group.[81]

The competent leaders rose rapidly. The example of Maurice Wilder-Neligan, from staff-sergeant at Gallipoli to commanding officer of his battalion in 1918, has been cited. Just one more of many other examples is that of Raymond Leane, born in 1878, who had left school at 12 years of age to become a shop-assistant. On landing at Gallipoli he was a captain commanding a company. Promoted to lieutenant colonel in Egypt, he was given command of the 48th Battalion, which he took to France. After recovering from a wound at Passchendaele he was promoted in June 1918 to command a brigade in the Hundred Days. By war's end he had a DSO and bar, MC and eight MID and was then awarded the CMG and CB. He went on to be Police Commissioner in SA and the founding president of Adelaide Legacy.

The leaders, contrary to legend, were becoming steadily younger. By 1918 the average age of commanders throughout the BEF at each strata from battalion to corps was ten years younger than it had been in 1914. In September 1918 the average age of corps commanders was 52.5 while Monash was 53. That of divisional commanders was 42, while in the AIF it was 40. The drop in age was the consequence of casualties, but also from the intense strain of combat which demanded young, more resilient minds and bodies. The majority of divisional commanders in September 1918 had been majors in 1914 (four steps in rank), while most brigade commanders had been captains. It was this younger generation of leaders who by 1918 had devised the tactics of the combined-arms battle with which to overwhelm the dominance of the defence.[82] It is strange to label this cohort of leaders as donkeys.

***

Early the next morning the 6th Brigade of the 2nd Division passed through its fellow brigade and, in savage fighting, finally cleared the crest of Mont St Quentin of Germans.[83] Meanwhile the 5th Division also began crossing the Somme and its 14th Brigade, following in the path of the 19th Battalion, swung around to the north of Peronne where, seizing an opportunity, it crossed the moat and scaled the walls to secure a foot-hold in the old town. The battle was concluded the following day when Peronne was cleared in heavy house-to-house fighting by 'Pompey' Elliott's 15th Brigade. With the fall of both the Mont and Peronne the battle turned into a slog to push the Germans back from the surrounding hills and the 'suburbs' of Peronne to its north.

The battle had cost the Australian Corps 3000 casualties and victory had been achieved without the support of tanks or creeping barrages. It was an infantry battle, characterized by intense, close combat, and had been decisively won by the Australian Corps against superior numbers. Credit for the victory can be widely apportioned. It was a 'soldiers' battle', and the Diggers had fought magnificently despite being dog-tired. They had been advancing and fighting for days with little chance of sleep or even rest. The adrenalin of combat can keep a soldier moving but we now know that, after 36 hours without sleep, mental performance has eroded by 50%, and after 72 hours the soldier has become an operational liability; he is essentially a walking zombie. Possibly if they had realized such consequences the WW1 commanders may have been more cautious in their demands. We should recognize that in the Hundred Days the Diggers usually went into battle already physically and mentally exhausted, but then usually triumphed. They did this decisively at Mont St Quentin.

It was a battle won by the junior leaders – the NCOs and the young officers were as equally tired as their soldiers but, by the unique nature of the battle, had to make decisions and assume far greater responsibility than was normally demanded of them. It was a very fluid battle and they responded by recognizing and grasping opportunities, and by keeping themselves and their tired men going. Mont St Quentin can be seen as the high point of Australian junior leadership in war.

***

Leadership 'is the art of influencing and directing men in tasks in such a way as to obtain their willing obedience, confidence, respect and loyal co-operation'.[84] Or more plainly, getting men to willingly do what they are told to do. The focus on leadership is recent. The officers of Marlborough and Wellington needed only a pointed finger and the order 'charge' to achieve their end, and the rigidly drilled red-coat responded. The need and importance of leadership grew in proportion to the dispersal of the soldiers on the battlefield. It was no longer the butt of the company sergeant-major's pike being shoved in his back that got the soldier forward. Now it was leadership that induced him to walk into no-mans-land with his rifle at the 'high port'. Surprisingly the BEF had little difficulty in this regard. When told to attack the Tommy climbed out of his trench and set out across no-mans-land.

Uniquely among the Allies, leadership within the BEF held firm while the French, Russian, Italian, and eventually the German armies, all suffered morale and leadership crises. The BEF succeeded despite the quite different styles of leadership within its various contingents, each devolving from the nature and ethos of the society from which it was drawn, ranging from the highly authoritarian style of the British to the *laissez-faire* of the Australians. It was sad that the higher British command was unable to appreciate that the AIF had a different, but equally effective, style of leadership, and that had the British approach had been imposed on the Diggers it could have had dire consequences. It is interesting to note that as Britain turned to conscription, and the social structure of the British Army altered, its style of leadership edged closer to that of the AIF.

***

Mont St Quentin had proved the soundness of Australian leadership. It had also proved the competence of its command. The leaders of the sections, platoons and companies had seized the opportunities and led their men with skill and determination. The commanders of the battalions, brigades and divisions had created the opportunities and marshaled the resources needed to win. Mont St Quentin shows the close relationship between leadership and command. The two words are closely related but are not synonymous. Command is the iron in the glove of leadership, in that it is the lawful authority vested in the leader, at each level of the military structure, with which he gets his subordinates to do their duty. It is command which lays down what will be done and how: it is then through leadership that it is achieved. In simplistic terms to lead is to inspire, to command is to direct and to mange is to organize. If we accept that leadership within the BEF was satisfactory, maybe British command was the intended target of the donkey shibboleth.

In 1914 the British higher command lacked the knowledge and

competency for total war on a continental scale. The experience of the British high command had been in small colonial wars fought to police the Empire. They were skilled at repressing mutiny (India), repelling native hordes (the Zulu War), extending and securing the boundaries of Empire (Afghanistan and the Sudan) and containing insurgency (the Boer War). In 1914 the British Army lacked the doctrine, tactics, organization and, above all, numbers for a Continental conflict. By comparison the Continental armies were vast. On the declaration of war Germany immediately mobilized 80 divisions while Britain initially could only deploy four of its total of eight infantry divisions to France, a force equivalent in combat power to the AIF by 1916. It was to the Kaiser the 'contemptible little army'. Yet within two years Britain had three million men under arms with 50 British and 11 dominion divisions fighting in France. Within a further two years it had devised the tactics and strategy, developed the technology and mastered the logistics to defeat its professional enemy and to humiliate the vaunted German General Staff. And this was achieved by a leadership which by popular public opinion was old, incompetent and decrepit. It took time for the generals to master the challenge, but considering the circumstances it was managed in a remarkably short space of time. The generals of the BEF not only adapted to the war but also transformed the way it was fought.

Command on earlier battlefields had been relatively simple. All that was needed was nerves of steel to stand on the highest ground and, while the cannon balls flew by, to direct the army below. From his vantage point the commander could both see the battle and control his subordinates: the WW1 general could do neither. His battlefield was too vast for him to see what was happening and he had to rely on reports from his subordinates, which by the time he received them were dated. Neither did he have reliable and timely means of directing their actions once battle had begun. He operated in a remarkably gloomier 'fog of war' than his present-day successors, who now face the antithesis of an information over-load. Hence it was a very significant step in the Learning Curve when the generals realized that delegation of command in battle was essential. In the early years of the war decision taking was tightly held at the highest level (which contributed to the catastrophic casualties). Yet, as the war progressed, experience and growing confidence in their subordinates saw command increasingly delegated. Monash, recognizing the constraints on his capacity to command at Mont St Quentin, delegated most of his authority to his subordinates once he had completed the deployment.

Mont St Quentin well illustrates the inter-play between command and leadership and the frustration that was apparent among the divisional and brigade commanders as they tried to read the battle as it unfolded. Bean records 'Pompey' Elliott often being forward of his battalion commanders in his effort to keep control and Bean also provides the following vignette that graphically illustrates the frustration even at the lowest level of the lack of communications. During the night of the 31st it was decided to bring down an artillery 'stonk' in the vicinity of a standing patrol of the 53rd Battalion commanded by a Lieutenant Waite. The patrol had to be recalled and several efforts were made, but all without success. Finally Private William Currey walked out into no-mans-land, cupped his hands and yelled 'Waitsy get in'. Bean then records: 'The Germans turned on him every weapon they had; he was gassed and his respirator was shot through. But Waite heard him and returned'.[85] As well as reflecting issues of command and control it is also instructive of leadership, initiative and discipline. Coincidently, Currey had also earned the Victoria Cross for his actions on the previous day and earlier the Military Medal and three bars.

The shortcomings of communications imposed particular restraints on command in WW1. The large immobile radios left the higher commanders 'chained' to their headquarters. The infamous 'chateaux generals', who supposedly never budged from the comfort and safety of their palaces, is well established folk-law and is a sub-set of the 'donkeys' legend. The statistics however, do not substantiate the claim: the chateaux failed to guarantee the safety of the generals. In the course of the war 78 British and Dominion generals were killed and 146 wounded.[86] Over half the Australian brigade commanders were wounded and two divisional commanders, Bridges and Holmes, were killed. Charles Rosenthal made a habit of being wounded; twice on Gallipoli and then as a brigadier-general at Pozieres in 1916. He was gassed at Passchendaele and then, after taking command of 2nd Division, was wounded once more at Hamel in 1918. 'Pompey' Elliott, hit in the buttocks by shrapnel at Mont St Quentin, famously gave the orders to his battalion commanders for the attack on Peronne standing, with his trousers down, while a medical orderly on his knees behind, dressed the wound.

***

The 'donkeys' shibboleth is one of the most widely quoted and also most facile. Popularised in the 1960s it reflected a failure to empathise with the past. The post-WW2 generation found Edwardian values strange. In photographs the generals looked stuffy and pompous, and must therefore have been incompetent. It is true that in the course of their learning many disastrous errors made and many lives were lost; inevitably, that is the nature of war. But learn they did, and with surprising speed, far quicker than did their enemy. It is now the armchair critics, usually with little military experience, who still cast this dated shibboleth. Those who continue to reproach should consider the five-fold burden that has always accompanied military command and always will. The commander works within the 'fog of war' with incomplete and unreliable information, and against an enemy seeking to outmanoeuvre and surprise him. He must make decisions based on incomplete information quickly and decisively while recognizing those decisions will involve the loss of soldiers' lives. He must have rigid control of his own fears and anxieties and set an example at all times of calmness and confidence. He must bear the burden of the 'loneliness of command' recognising and accepting that the ultimate responsibility for failure and for the loss of life will be his. He must have the resilience to accept and adapt to confusion, set-backs, delays and crises. This the generals of the BEF achieved. And they also managed to win the war.

CHAPTER 8

The Hindenburg Line

'The Lovable Larrikin'

Discipline

'Good-morning; good-morning!' The General said
When we met him last week on the way to the line.
Now the soldiers he smiled at are most of 'em dead,
And we're cursing his staff for incompetent swine.
'He's a cheery old card', grunted Harry to Jack
As they slogged up to Arras with rifle and pack.
...
But he did for them both by his plan of attack.

Siegfried Sassoon[87]

What was to have been the Germans' Winter Line fell in early autumn. To the north the New Zealand Division had taken Bapaume, and Arras had fallen to the Canadians. With the loss of Mount St Quentin Ludendorff had no option than to order the twenty kilometre withdrawal to the Hindenburg Line. Against a persistent German rear-guard, the pursuit, which for the Australian Corps began on 5 September, was over rolling open hills and wide marshy valleys. By 10 September they had advanced to the trenches of the old British Reserve Line and in front of them lay the 1917 battlefield, firstly with its old British Main and Outpost Lines and their belts of rusted wire obstacles. And beyond that, on the hill crest, lay what was called the German Outpost Line.

The Hindenburg, or to the Germans the Siegfried Line, was the most comprehensive defensive position developed until that time, and it was also the sole remaining established defensive barrier before the German frontier. It had been progressively developed through 1916 and 1917, and therein lay both its great strength and two critical shortcomings.[88] While it reflected years of development it also carried outdated concepts of a series of linear defences rather than the newer approach of scattered and mutually supporting strongpoints. But its greatest weakness was its devotion to the concept of 'defence of the reverse slope'. Early in the war, as the effectiveness of artillery had improved, it was thought better to hide the main defences from view behind a lightly held hill line. For the Hindenburg Line that lightly held, or Outpost Line, was to be the ridge in front of the St Quentin Canal behind which the German Main Line defences had been developed.

Realisation then dawned that if the lightly held Outpost Line fell the main defences would then be overlooked from the heights above and be vulnerable to direct and observed fire. Recognising this weakness the Germans worked hard through 1918 to re-develop the Outpost Line on the ridge into a new Main Line and to push their Outpost Line forward into what had been the old British trenches. Essentially they shifted the centre of gravity forward and deepened the Hindenburg defences. This led to a defensive position seven to nine kilometres deep, containing five or more defensive lines. It was seemingly impregnable. Even if the new Outpost and Main lines fell, and the defences were overlooked from the ridge, there remained the old Main Line and, in front of it, the St Quentin Canal. The Canal, with steep fifteen-metre banks, water two-metres deep and ten-metres wide, was a daunting obstacle. There was, however, a point directly opposite the Australian advance where the Canal ran for five and a half kilometres through a tunnel. The ground above was the obvious approach and hence drew heavier defences than elsewhere, with an extra three lines of trenches and wire obstacles hundreds of metres deep.

***

By mid-September the 1st and 4th Divisions, which had been resting after their exertions in the savage post-Amiens battles of 9–14 August, returned to make the initial attacks on the Hindenburg Line. Rawlinson launched his Army in an assault on the Outpost line on 18 September.[89] As at Amiens it was a dawn attack that began at 5.40 am, supported by tanks and a creeping barrage by 1600 guns. The Australian Corps attacked in the centre, flanked by III Corps on its north and IX Corps to its south. Only eight tanks were available to assist the Australians but their paucity was compensated by massing 200 medium machine-guns and using their indirect fire to supplement the barrage. It had rained during the night leaving a morning mist, which was thickened by a weight of smoke shells in the barrage. The Australians quickly took the first and second objectives of the old British Main and Outpost lines.

From around 9 am the battalions were arriving on the second objective. The third objective, the German Outpost (cum new Main) Line, was to be taken by 'exploitation' if possible but no plans for a deliberate attack had been prepared. Without the cover of a barrage the 1st Division pushed on uphill using fire and movement and seizing every opportunity as it arose. By 10.30 am it had started to reach the crest and now overlooked the Saint Quentin Canal and by 12.30 had occupied most of its Phase 3 objective. On their right the 4th Division faced deep and uncut wire obstacles that stopped its progress. They waited until evening and at 10.55 pm Raymond Leane's 12th Brigade attacked behind a creeping barrage. Although the barrage did little damage to the wire it held down the German heads while it was negotiated by small parties. Remarkably these small scattered groups of the 46th and 48th Battalions, clambering up the hill, were attacking at least nine German battalions, which they drove from their trenches. Having secured the crest the 46th Battalion then bombed its way north along the trench line until it met its sister battalion from the 1st Division, the 14th Battalion, working its way south. The Australians had seized a key part of the Hindenburg Line. In the process they had taken 4,300 prisoners and captured 76 guns at the cost of 1,260 casualties.

For Rawlinson's Army it had been a day of mixed fortunes. Once more the techniques of the combined-arms battle had triumphed. The combination of creeping barrage and tanks got most of the infantry forward. The German artillery defensive fire had been minimal for two reasons. Again the 4th Army had been favoured by mist to supplement its smoke screen but it also had the advantage of the detailed map of the defences, albeit dated February 1917, captured by the armoured cars at Amiens. In consequence the counter-battery fire had been precise and deadly. The Australians by the end of the day had reached all of their objectives; the IX Corps would shortly do so; only III Corps had failed.

Once more the Australians had achieved a great feat of arms and, unbeknown to themselves, had broken their way into the new Main Hindenburg Line, which while recognized by the Germans as a catastrophic loss was largely unacknowledged by the Allies, who were yet to realize its tactical significance. To their north, however, III Corps had failed to take even its second objective and, after a succession of piecemeal divisional attacks, decided to launch a coordinated corps attack at dawn on 21 September. Rawlinson directed that the 1st Division support this endeavour. The 1st and 3rd Battalions were allocated to the task and it was to precipitate the most serious crisis in discipline faced by the AIF.

***

Military discipline exists for two reasons: firstly, to ensure that in great danger the soldier does not surrender to his instinct for self-preservation, and secondly, to keep order within the army so that it can achieve its purpose. The nature of the discipline that can be imposed on soldiers is reflective of the character of the society from which they are drawn. Tight discipline could be imposed on the Tommy, coming from a society with a rigid class structure in which 'each knew his place' and from a tightly ordered industrial workplace. On the other hand, by 1918, in the 130 years since settlement, there had been a shift from British attitudes in Australia. A different society had evolved with its own national character. Five features reflect that Australian character which made a hurdle to establishing conventional military discipline. A Digger is challenging ('who says?'), fraternal ('on ya mate'), egalitarian ('up there Cazaly'), laconic ('she'll be alright'), and righteous ('give a bloke a fair go'), and for it to be effective Australian discipline has to respect these traits. It took time for the AIF to come to grips with discipline and it can be marked by three distinct steps.

The first could be described as its infancy which lasted from the formation of the AIF until it deployed to the Western Front after Gallipoli. This period saw order evolve out of the initial chaos and the creation of a unique Australian discipline that served not only the AIF but the Australian Army ever since. After the outbreak of the war, and with the government decision to raise a separate force for overseas service, there was a rapid response. The recruits had begun pouring into the camps from 8 August 1914 and onto the troopships from 21 September. Remarkably in that time 18,000 men had joined, been kitted, organized into their units and given the barest rudiments of individual training.

They reflected the breadth of Australian society. While friends, relatives and neighbours joined, most made an individual decision so that the members of the battalions as they formed were largely made up of strangers thrown together for the first time. The most marked characteristic of the force was its youth. Most were under 25 years of age and carried the wildness and irresponsibility of the young. There was an excitement and exuberance at the great adventure that challenged efforts to impose discipline and constraints on their behaviour.

While the small regular army and the militia provided the senior ranks the junior leadership was largely selected on the basis of who was available. A few brought experience from the cadets and the militia, some had past service, but often the junior leaders were chosen on the basis of whoever looked the part. Often they were reluctant nominees, unwilling to stand above or impose discipline. Problems were compounded by the loose recruiting procedures. The medical examination, which was quite exacting, was the only hurdle to enlistment. There were no record or character checks which meant that many who were quite unsuitable to be soldiers were enlisted: men with criminal records of violence, disorder and theft were accepted.

This largely leaderless mass of men from disparate backgrounds and with varying motivations had to be welded into a fighting force. There were probably only two positive factors: the wild and at times uncontrollable enthusiasm could be channelled into a willingness to work together, and there was a very small leavening of experienced ex-soldiers together with a few very competent officers to pass on their knowledge. Behaviour, however, was generally abysmally bad. The reports of conduct on the first convoy and then in the camps in Egypt are depressing. Wild misbehaviour was characterized by well-publicized riots in the Wazza, Cairo's brothel district, and rampant AWOL. Eventually 133 of the worst, defined by Bean as 'the wasters', had to be sent home as unfit to serve. This state of semi-anarchy was brought to a sudden halt by the reality of battle.

Gallipoli was a catalyst in a sudden change of behaviour. It was only through its exuberance and energy, rather than military competence or discipline, that the AIF survived the landing. Battle was a sobering experience and very quickly the men of the AIF came to realize survival depended on leadership, training and also discipline. On Gallipoli the natural leaders came to the fore and so did the foundations of the unique code of conduct that suits the Australian character. The men on Gallipoli were a different breed from their Tommy cousins. Conventional military discipline was not what got the Anzacs to jump the bags at the Neck, to toss the bombs back at Quinn's Post, or drop into the Turkish trenches at Lone Pine. The motivation had more to do with the five features of Australian character. Discipline had to arrive at an accommodation with these traits without compromising its primary purpose. It seems that is what happened.

A unique and even now unspoken contract between the soldier and the leader began to evolve: 'I will tolerate your behaviour as long as you keep it within bounds' to which the response was 'I will accept your commands as long as you keep them within bounds'. Once the parameters were established the men adapted quickly. The law ceased trying to be all-encompassing and the army ceased being 'nanny' to every moment of the soldier's day. It was a code of conduct that respected the worth of the individual.

The men who came out of Gallipoli were a more mature group than the youngsters who had gone in. As the two divisions expanded to four and began intense training for France there was a notable change in the tone of their conduct. Their recent experience, and now their anticipation of what was to come, steadied their exuberance. There was an acceptance at last of the need for discipline and the unspoken code of conduct that had evolved offered a foundation. It accommodated and supported another feature of the relationship between the Australian Army and its soldiers. It encouraged him to be 'a thinking soldier' who contributes positively to what is happening around him. The army does not want a mindless automaton simply responding to the orders of his leaders. The Digger is encouraged to think, reason, question; and to contribute his ideas, but he is then expected to respond immediately to a command when it is given. When this became the ethos of the AIF it motivated the soldiers to step forward as leaders and in a crisis to think and react without awaiting an order. This placed the Digger in marked contrast with the Tommy, whose initiative was not necessarily encouraged. It was an attitude that undoubtedly played a part in the combat effectiveness of the AIF.

***

They were very different soldiers who landed in Marseilles in mid-1916 from the young men who had clambered ashore a year earlier at Anzac Cove. They arrived with the basis of their discipline established but far from settled. The second phase of its evolution had begun and would extend for the next 18 months until they came out of Passchendaele. Discipline in France in the early days was characterized by unruliness reflected in the minor offences of drunkenness, gambling and absence-without-leave. From their arrival the Diggers established their own interpretation of which military laws mattered and which didn't. It reflected their independence of outlook. Who could blame them for drunkenness under the circumstance they faced, and particularly when booze and gambling was affordable with their comparatively high pay? AWOL was simply extending the pleasure of their leave, or taking a break when the individual deemed he needed it. What distinguished it from desertion was the intent of returning to duty in due course.

They believed they had strong justification for their recalcitrance. The 'barrack-room lawyers' had ready excuses. 'We had signed up for the duration, little expecting that the duration would extend year after long year. We consider ourselves civilians in uniform to whom the full weight of military justice should not apply. While we have spells of leave in France and England, there is no home leave, so surely there is no harm if we extend the miserable leave we are granted. As front-line soldiers surely we are entitled to less rigorous discipline when out of the trenches. As time passes and recruiting begins to dry up, our numbers grow fewer and the demands grow heavier, surely we could be rewarded with fewer rules and regulations'. However, their self-defined interpretation of military law had its consequences.

The incarceration rate of the Diggers was at one stage seventeen times higher than the rest of the BEF.[90] At times British military prisons contained more Diggers than they held Tommies. Haig complained that one in every hundred Australian soldiers was in jail. The alternative view to that of the barrack-room lawyer was that the unruliness was hurting the combat effectiveness of the AIF. Their attitude to 'good order and military discipline' meant a serious drain on the manpower of the Australian Corps, at times the equivalent of up to two brigades worth of soldiers were in prison. They imposed a heavy burden on their mates, who in their absence were forced to carry the extra load.

An associated issue was the prevalence of venereal disease. There had been 6000 cases of VD in Egypt of whom 1344 had to be returned to Australia: that is, two battalions worth of soldiers.[91] In France in 1917 the rate was 144 per thousand while the British was 24[92] and it remained steady at around ten times that of the British Army. In the course of the war the AIF suffered 55,000 cases. Its prevalence can be attributed to the lack of home leave and the relatively high pay rates of the Australians. Reputedly, seven of the VC winners bore the scars. While it takes little imagination to recognise how desperately some men needed solace after their experience in the trenches, it had its consequences. There was the inevitable operational impact; recovery needed at least a month of treatment. The high incidence translated into reduced fighting strength.

The Australian public had been aware of the misbehaviour since the riots in the Wazza in Cairo and had tried to excuse it as misplaced high spirits. Now that the Diggers were in France and taking leave in Britain their bad behaviour drew increasingly attention. The public faced the conundrum that while they were proud of the Digger's battlefield achievements they were embarrassed by his behaviour when out of the line. Rather than condemning it they sought to excuse it by trivializing its seriousness. They chose the shibboleth of the 'lovable larrikin' to make light of the embarrassment. Yet it was the larrikin who was the cause of the problem.

'Larrikin' is a word popularly believed to be of uniquely Australian origin, derived from the brogue of an Irish copper reporting someone as 'larking about'. However, it may have its roots in the Warwickshire dialect where 'larriken' is a mischievous youth. It is urban slang and was usually associated with 'the push', the gangs of city hooligans that plagued Sydney and Melbourne pre-war. It was a convenient word with which to excuse those Diggers whose unruly behaviour, when out of the line, caused wide irritation.

Often cited as the classic image of the larrikin Digger is the famous photo by Frank Hurley of Private John (Barney) Hines, taken at the end of the battle of Polygon Wood in 1917. He sits surrounded by the loot he had taken from German prisoners. Twice wounded and responsible for the capture single handed of 60 Germans at Messines, he was a valourous soldier. He was also convicted of nine breaches of discipline and is suspected of having robbed the bank in Amiens. Was Hines more trouble than he was worth, or was it his independent spirit that made him a valuable combat soldier? And how typical was he? He was in fact the antithesis of the larrikin: he was middle-aged and a 'loner', and post-war led the life of a recluse.

Private 'Barney' Hines with his loot at Polygon Wood, September 1917. Larrikin or loner?
Source: AWM E00822

***

Broadly there are four reasons for misbehaviour. It can be from over-excitement and uncontrolled exuberance. This accounts for the behaviour of the young men of the AIF until matured by the reality of combat on Gallipoli. Secondly, it may be rebellion against restraints placed on his behaviour. This can be seen to be the reaction of the larrikins in the early days in France as they bucked against military authority. Thirdly, it may be for gain, flowing from opportunity or inclination. The criminals who were Bean's 'wasters' who stole from their mates were soon identified and removed, or in some instances continued their brigandage in the French countryside after deserting. Fourthly, it can be the consequence of being over-extended, pushed to the extreme of their physical and emotional strength to the point of breakdown or rebellion. This is what faced the Australian Corps in 1918.

The third phase of the evolution of the unique Australian discipline was in 1918 as the Australian Corps swung to the offensive. A degree of disorder had been appearing as a result of the punishing losses from the battles of 1917. It showed itself in the serious offence of desertion which increased in 1918. Usually desertion is associated with the collapse of morale, signalling the fracturing of an army. This was obviously not the case in the AIF in 1918 which bore high desertion concurrently with high morale. Yet the Australian Corps in 1918 was suffering desertion at ten times the rate of the British.[93] Hundreds of Diggers were lurking in English towns and French villages. But by then these were not only wasters or larrikins extending their leave, but desperate men who were no longer able to face the trauma of the battlefield.

Too seldom do we reflect on what the battlefield held and its impact on the soldiers. There was severe stress, even in the quiet times in the trenches, always the fear, the lack of sleep, and the imagining. In 1918 the Australian Corps was constantly on the offensive. We should consider the effect on the Diggers of those attacks. They would be advancing within twenty-five metres of the barrage in a world darkened by the dirt and mud thrown up, swirling smoke lit by the flashes of the exploding shells and streaked by tracer of passing machine gun fire. A cacophony of noise would be hammering their senses. There was the roar of battle with the thump of exploding shells, the chatter of the machine guns, crack of rifle fire, cries of those hit. They would have had the pervading putrid stench of faeces and rotting corpses overlaid with pungent smells of cordite, mustard gas, dust and smoke. And all the time the ground under them was shuddering with the impact of the barrage: the air around them rippling with the blast of the exploding shells and the whiplash passing of bullets and shrapnel. Above all there was the horror of the killing, with death often very close and personal.[94] Words have never been able to do justice to the horror of battle, and the World War 1 battlefield must have been the most horrible. And into that hell they walked again and again over the months, with the only escape of becoming a casualty. Although they would not run away from the battlefield often the thought of returning to it was too much to bear. That some buckled under the stress was inevitable: that more did not is remarkable.

The war saw a tidal change in the tempo of battle. Waterloo was fought in a day; now battles were interminable and the demand on the physical and mental stamina of the participants was huge. A new phenomenon of combat stress or battle fatigue, which they dubbed 'shell shock', was recognized but only vaguely understood. That it was impacting on the effectiveness of the men was apparent but its cause was little understood and its treatment was rudimentary. Subsequently it has been exhaustively examined and it is now recognized that all men are ultimately subject to it. There is a famous US Army statistic of WW2 that after 60 days of constant combat 98% will have become psychiatric casualties while the other 2% would have already had 'aggressive psychotic personalities', that is, they were crazy before they got there.[95]

Related to this are studies showing combat effectiveness is at its greatest in the period from ten to twenty days after entering combat. The initial days are spent in adjusting and adapting to the threat and then, after the plateau, there is a steady decline into ineffectiveness.[96] Instinctively, as they lacked analysis, the BEF adapted to the situation. In the static phase of trench warfare, units were rotated through a cycle of three to five days in each of the front, reserve and depth lines and then after approximately three months, given rest well behind the lines. Even with the demands of the Hundred Days Monash tried to find the Diggers relief from the constant combat. As has been seen, the divisions alternated in roughly ten-day cycles between rest and combat. The failure of the US Army to follow this practice in WW2 led to a ratio of battle to psychiatric casualties of up to 1:1. Several factors saved the AIF from an equivalent fate; principally being its team cohesion and the bond of mate-ship between the Diggers. The WW2 US Army operated as a machine while the WW1 AIF was, by comparison, a family. It did not save all from the longer-term effect of the stress.

All who had been in combat carried the emotional scars but some suffered worse. Recognition of post-traumatic stress disorder is recent. It is now acknowledged that 15% of those who have had the experience of 'close-range, interpersonal, aggressive confrontation', looking into the eyes of someone with the intent of killing you or whom you must kill, will suffer long-term emotional consequences.[97] Its symptoms may become quickly apparent or surface years later. Unrecognised by the community, this stress from the war took a savage long-term toll on the veterans; among many being 'Pompey' Elliott, who committed suicide in 1931.

The consequence of the horror can be seen in the photographs of the Diggers taken while resting after their battles. In most cases they are very drawn faces but it is in the eyes that the stress tells. There is a much shown photograph, sent to the Provost Marshal, as an act of bravado, by a group of deserters. Some, looking at it, would applaud that bravado, others would find the photograph infinitely sad; fine young men who had buckled under the terrible stress and who were unable to continue. Their only escape was desertion or a self-inflicted wound. Remarkably only 710 are recorded as taking the latter course.[98] Conversely several thousand deserted. While some were wasters and larrikins who formed into gangs of thugs, raping and looting in the French countryside, many would have been soldiers who had simply reached the end of their tether. Despite the bravado of their act there is a well of sadness and confusion in the eyes of most of those in that photograph. They had reached the point where they were unable to continue but they would have received scant sympathy or understanding. For most of those who broke there would be little more than a cup of tea, a pat on the back and to be sent back to the line. If they ran they could expect a court martial and jail or, for many Tommies, a firing squad.[99] It was only towards the end that there was realization that combat stress could be as wounding as bullets and shrapnel.

***

Among the senior officers it was the commander of the 5th Division, Major General Talbot Hobbs, who in July, shortly after Hamel, was the first to

The deserters' taunting photo to the Assistant Provost Marshal. Criminals or cripples? Source: AWM A03862

recognize that many of the soldiers charged with desertion were nervous wrecks and directed his battalion commanders to interview these men individually. While Monash supported this initiative others, including several Australian generals of the AIF, still believed the high desertion rate and ill-discipline in the Australian Corps was in consequence of the refusal to impose the death penalty. Otherwise subject to the same scales of offences and punishments as the British Army, the death penalty was confined by Australian military law to guilt of mutiny, desertion to the enemy, or treason, and even then could only be imposed with the confirmation of the Governor General. Despite this provision 121 were sentenced to death by Australian courts martial, of which the majority, 104, were for desertion. Not one was executed. Only three Australians went to the firing squad or the gallows in the course of the war: two, serving with NZEF, for desertion, and one by a British court for murder.

There is ongoing debate as to whether the comparatively low British crime rate was the consequence of a fear of the death penalty or was due to subservience to a rigid class structure or the acculturation of an industrialized work-force. In any case it did not endow the Tommy with greater morale or combat effectiveness. The counter debate is whether the perceived Australian ill-discipline was the consequence of the lack of a death penalty, the product of a more egalitarian society or the fact that the men were worn out and their team-cohesion was coming apart. Yet in comparison to both his enemy and all other participants, the Digger sustained remarkably high morale. Why?

This is a question which takes us back to considerations of morale and esprit de corps, leadership and confidence in their tactics and battlecraft. It seems these things held the Corps together in the face of exhaustion and disciplinary issues that could have otherwise torn it apart. Yet not all desertion was as serious as it may initially appear. There is the instance of Private Walter Schwarz who, tired of the ridicule of his name, deserted in England in 1916, then enlisted in the Royal Fusiliers where he was commissioned and finished the war as a lieutenant with an MC and bar and three MID. He was eventually pardoned for his desertion by the Governor General.

***

While desertion carries a stigma, it is trumped by the seriousness of mutiny. Where desertion is the action of an individual, mutiny is collective and can become contagious. The thought of mutiny, the mass refusal to obey orders, sends a shudder through all armies. Yet this is what confronted the Australian Corps in September 1918. During the years of static trench warfare there had been regular and rostered periods of rest, but with the Hundred Days there was constant movement and frequent battle. It is apparent that Monash was aware of the demands on the Diggers and after Amiens worked the Corps as two teams, alternating the 1st and 4th Divisions with the 2nd, 3rd and 5th Divisions on approximately ten-day 'shifts'. Yet in that ten-day period for day after day half the Corps was either advancing or deploying into quick attacks. There was little sleep or rest for any, from private to general. Monash's strategic grasp enabled him to see that the Germans had reached the tipping point and unremitting pressure could lead to their collapse. Hence he drove the Diggers on, but nearly to the point of their, and his own, collapse through exhaustion. Eventually there were signs that units could fracture. No longer was the stress confined to individuals, forcing them to the point of desertion, but a far more serious face of group disorder was appearing: mutiny – 'collective insubordination, resistance to military authority, colluding to resist or inciting others to resist'.

The 1st Battalion had performed with great valour on 18 September, and against the odds had seized its third objective, part of the new Main Hindenburg Line. III Corps on its left had failed once more to reach even its second objective.[100] Once more the Australian Corps was to go to its rescue and help it to do what it could not do on its own. On 19 September the Battalion, after it had been relieved, was making its way to rest when it was stopped and told of a change of plans that meant it was to join an attack the following day to take the III Corps' second objective. Some refused and 127 made their way to the rear. At dawn the next day the remaining 10 officers and 83 other ranks of the Battalion attacked as ordered. They achieved the Battalion's objective, secured their designated part of III Corps' second objective, and took 120 prisoners for the loss of three killed and 42 wounded.

It could be interpreted that the actions of the rebels was something more akin to industrial action than mutiny. They argued that it was an unreasonable demand – being called on to put their lives on the line to salve the reputation of a poor British formation which couldn't or wouldn't do its own job, and which in the past had repeatedly failed to give the Diggers support when needed. It is easy to understand, if not condone, their resentment. One can almost feel their self-righteous anger. Once more they were to 'bail out the Pommies' just as they had done so many times before. They would have recalled the casualties their battalion had sustained when III Corps had failed to take Chipilly on 8 or 9 August until their Staff Sergeant Hayes showed them how.

The 1st Battalion had suffered 123 casualties on 18 September, the highest of any of the 15 Australian battalions involved, and now they were to suffer more. Adding to their anger was the fact that they had already been relieved, and were on their way back to a well earned rest, when the order was changed. What too was the effect on their morale when around 40 of the Battalion, who had been at Gallipoli, were finally granted leave back in Australia and departed on 13 September? Was there celebration at their comrades' good fortune or was it tinged with envy and resentment at the loss of their numbers at such a critical time. The Battalion probably entered the battle on 18 September with fewer than 350 all ranks, of whom a third had since become casualties. Then in the time following the battle there had been little time for rest or sleep. Also the company largely involved in the mutiny had lost all but two of its officers on 18 September, and with tragic irony these two both became casualties on 20 September from a random shell while negotiating with the rebels.

Their commanding officer, Lieutenant Colonel B.V. (Bertie) Stacy, believed the mutiny stemmed from 'over-mention of the troops in newspapers, so that they over-valued themselves'. This was a harsh judgement and also a back-handed criticism of Monash's efforts to get greater recognition for the achievements of the Diggers. Conversely, there may have been a feeling of resentment among the Diggers that their effort was still not getting the recognition it deserved. Stacy, a hard task master, also believed that the mutiny was incited by 'trouble makers'. From this distance in time it is difficult to judge. Was it a one-off incident or did it presage a looming crisis for the Australian Corps?

Of the mutineers 25 were NCOs, three had been awarded the MM, nearly half had been previously wounded, and several had suffered shell-shock. In due course all were charged with mutiny but the courts martial must have found mitigating circumstances. Eleven were found not guilty, and one guilty only of being AWOL. The remaining 115 were found guilty of the lesser charge of desertion rather than of mutiny and were sentenced to three to five years penal servitude. It is of note that while over half had clean conduct sheets, six of those guilty had previously accumulated a total of 46 disciplinary charges against them. Stacy firmly believed these were the men who incited the mutiny, but opinions differ. There are those who saw the battalion as reaching the point of exhaustion. Then to the chagrin of the Battalion, in the days that followed, until the court martial could be convened, the recalcitrants were made to traipse behind the Battalion as it moved. They were like an albatross hung around its neck or a leper's bell to the pride and dignity of the 1st Battalion.

There are two other recorded instances of mutiny at the time. Following their victory in clearing Peronne on 5 September three platoons of the 59th Battalion refused to resume the advance, claiming exhaustion and the need for rest. Their brigade commander, 'Pompey' Elliott, intervened and convinced them to rejoin their battalion. Then on 25 September 13 men of the 3rd Australian Tunneling Company refused to go to the front. Were these isolated instances of mutiny or were they the warning-bell of the coming collapse of the Corps? Monash, and his Canadian counterpart Currie, were driving their respective corps mercilessly. Monash was also driving himself, and was probably on the threshold of breakdown when the Corps came out of the line on 5 October. The eventual collapse of unit cohesion was inevitable, but was it imminent?

***

Even before the battle of 18 September the planning for the next phase was in hand.[101] In a display of confidence Rawlinson delegated the task to Monash whose concept was to launch the two US divisions that were temporarily under his command in an attack from the German Outpost Line to secure the tunnel zone. Two Australian divisions would then pass through and secure the Support Line in depth beyond the tunnel zone. There were two risks to this plan. Firstly it was to be an assault on a very narrow five-and-a-half kilometre front, the width of the canal tunnel, where lay the heaviest concentration of German defences. Rawlinson intervened, and fortuitously arranged for IX Corps to attempt a concurrent crossing of the canal to the south. The second, and major, risk to Monash's plan, however, was that the start-line of the northern US division was the old III Corps third objective of 18 September, which still remained in German hands.

Once more the guns played an important part in the battle, contributing with both positive and negative effect. That an attack was imminent was obvious to the Germans. As there was little point to secrecy, which had figured so emphatically at Amiens, and with so many guns and copious shells available, a preliminary bombardment was to be laid lasting four days from 25 September. This barrage, which included 30,000 mustard gas shells in their first use by the British, fell heavily on the tunnel zone, no longer with the intent of 'destruction', but rather to cut the heavy wire obstacles and to seal the defenders in their deep bunkers. Counter-battery fire, with observation from the ridge and the aid of the captured map, was devastating to the German guns, which then contributed little to the battle. As had become customary, any assault that kept close to the creeping barrage succeeded, but where the infantry lost contact it invariably failed. Sadly this was again the case on the northern flank.

In a preliminary operation on the 27 September the US 27th Division attempted to seize its start-line, which had been III Corps' infamous third objective of 18 September, which was still in German hands. It attacked in fog and soon lost the creeping barrage. There were conflicting reports of partial success that meant few knew where the men of the 27th were after the battle and it was feared they were scattered in isolated groups across the battlefield. This failure and then confusion meant that, when the main attack was launched on 29 September, the left flank had still to secure its start-line but it could not be provided with a creeping barrage for fear of shelling the remnants of the earlier attack. The other ingredient for a successful combined arms battle was frustrated when the accompanying tanks ran into a minefield and were lost. Inevitably the attack failed and, in the process, the US 27th Division and the following Australian 3rd Division became entangled.

The failure of the left flank was widely attributed to the inexperience of the US 27th Division. This overlooks the original failure of III Corps on 18 September and of its subsequent unsuccessful efforts. It is also significant that this was the one area of the Hindenburg Line where the Germans applied the new concept of mutually supporting strong-points rather than linear defence. Here they relied on the ruins of two heavily fortified farmhouse complexes, Gillemont and Quennemont farms, which held out until late in the afternoon of 29 September, thereby partly frustrating Monash's plan.

Meanwhile, on the right, the US 30th Division, attacking from the start-line secured by the Australians on 18 September, and keeping with its creeping barrage, reached its objective on the tunnel zone. The 5th Division then passed through and, although enfiladed because of the failure on its left flank, managed to reach its objective of the Support Line beyond the canal tunnel. Rather than a fist firmly in the guts of the Support Line all that had been achieved was a very vulnerable finger-hold that could be readily chopped off. But succour came from a surprise direction. Four kilometres to the south the 46th Midlands Division of IX Corps, under the heaviest concentration of artillery of the war, crossed the canal using extraordinary ingenuity: rafts, life-boats, ropes, and even life-belts from the Channel ferries were employed. The weight and density of the barrage moving ahead of them pulverized the approaches to the canal, then its banks, and finally the German defences on the far bank. By 3 pm the 46th was securely across and the 32nd Division passed through to penetrate the Support Line and to then secure the exposed right flank of the 5th Division.

With the main objective secured, the attacks by 4th Army over the next few days degenerated into the customary rolling maul, formations making isolated and poorly supported thrusts with heavy losses and little gain. The guns needed time to re-locate and to re-register, replacement tanks had to be ferried forward, headquarters had to refocus and re-start the planning process. Yet by 3 October the 4th Army was able to launch a well-planned and supported attack by 2nd Division, together with the British 32nd and 46th Divisions on a front of eleven kilometres, supported by 38 tanks and a heavy concentration of planned artillery fire. Once more the systematic combined-arms battle triumphed. The assault over-ran the last of the Hindenburg defences, the Beaurevoir Line, to a depth of two kilometres.

11th Brigade with US soldiers and British tanks clearing the 'tunnel roof' on 29 September 1918. Source: AWM K00114

***

The fighting days of the AIF were drawing to a close. On the explicit orders of Prime Minister W.M. (Billy) Hughes, laid down months earlier, the Corps had to be withdrawn for rest by 5 October. Was he prescient in seeing that as the date when the Hindenburg Line would be finally over-run, two months after Amiens, and when the Diggers were reaching the point of exhaustion? His motive, of course, believing the war could not end until late 1919, was to keep the AIF operational until its conclusion. Having the Corps fighting until the end would give him his bargaining chip for an Australian seat at the peace negotiations. It was a motive that could be seen as either ego driven or one to ensure Australia, and particularly the Diggers, received the reward for its effort. If the Diggers had failed militarily from exhaustion, or worse, the collapse of discipline, their efforts and sacrifice would have been in vain. But whether the war would be won in years or weeks, the Corps had reached the point where rest had to be given. Undisputedly they were desperately tired, but was their discipline in peril? There had been three cases of mutiny involving fewer than 200 men out of 50,000, which is 1/250th of the force: hardly a significant number.

Concurrently there was another mutiny running its course that refuted any perception of the break-down of unit cohesion or esprit. The strength of the Corps was declining significantly in consequence of the heavy casualties and the fall off in recruiting. It was not a circumstance unique to the AIF. All armies, even the conscript armies, were all facing the reality that, after the slaughter of four years of war, men were becoming scarce. German, British and French battalions were all fighting with numbers reduced to critical levels. In the British army brigades of four battalions had been reduced to three. For the AIF to keep its brigades at somewhere near fighting strength they would have to follow suit. Already in March three battalions had been disbanded and their men re-allocated. By September it became imperative to break up more battalions. When the decision was announced between 20 and 23 September it led to the most widespread rebellion suffered by the AIF. The men of the eight nominated battalions refused to obey the order to disband. Approximately 15% of the infantry were involved, technically in a mutiny, but with the encouragement of their fellow Diggers and the sympathy of their leaders.

When the 19th, 21st, 25th, 29th, 37th, 42nd, 54th and 60th Battalions were separately called to parade and were told of their disbandment the men refused, with the exception of the 60th which bowed to the authority of its brigade commander, 'Pompey' Elliott. After their officers and senior NCOs had departed they 'soldiered on' under elected leaders, usually the most competent of the corporals. Rigid discipline and exact military routine was maintained. Rations destined for other battalions 'fell off the back of wagons' as they passed the gates of the recalcitrants. All they asked was to be allowed to go into the battle of the Hindenburg Line as they were. Eventually Monash conceded and granted a two-week reprieve. Once out of the line after 5 October the disbandments proceeded without rancour. No charges were ever laid.

Their action reflected fierce loyalty to their battalion. It should be borne in mind that none of these battalions was more than four years old. Here were no centuries of tradition, no regimental colours emblazoned with battle honours of Blenheim, Waterloo or Inkerman, no regimental silver and ancient traditions and ritual. Even the oldest of these battalions was less than four years of age and few of the soldiers would have been with their battalion for even that short time – that was assured by the casualty toll. But it was 'their battalion and no one would muck with it lightly'. The discipline of soldiers, with this degree of loyalty and devotion to the team and their comrades, was not likely to come unstuck quickly. Ironically it is the disbandment mutiny that shows the morale and the discipline of the AIF at its very highest. Yes, they were tired but given rest, there was 'a lot of fight in the old dog yet'.

***

By late on 3 October the battle for the Hindenburg Line was over. All five main belts of its defences had been over-run. The Fourth Army paused, restructured and prepared for the next foray. The US II Corps was to replace the Australian Corps when it came out of the line to rest, but it could not come forward until the very day of Billy Hughes deadline, 5 October. Rather than waste a good asset, or have troops sit idle, Rawlinson demanded one last effort from the Diggers.

The defended village of Montbrehain blocked the advance of Fourth Army. The 6th Brigade of 2nd Division remained the sole Australian formation that had not been committed in the Hindenburg operation. The 2nd Pioneer Battalion, reassigned to its secondary role as infantry, came forward on the night of 4/5 October and took over the line facing Montbrehain and behind it the 21st and 24th Battalions of 6th Brigade went into their assembly areas.

The battle bore the hallmarks of an Australian Corps operation. It was a dawn attack behind a creeping barrage from six Australian field artillery brigades (field regiments) and sadly, as customary with unregistered guns, there were casualties from 'drop-shorts'. A further two artillery brigades provided counter-battery fire, and the infantry advanced supported by twelve tanks. Fighting in the village was confused by the presence of a number of French civilians. A party of twenty women and children were so relieved at their release that they sought to remain with the attacking troops. There was too the distraction of 'liberating' a pile of barrels of beer.

The Pioneers, following the assaulting battalions, fought magnificently. When pinned down by German machine-gun fire a group moved to seize the position protecting the German flank. Then, bringing forward two Vickers guns, they enfiladed the Germans, and were able to bring their fire onto the enemy, killing 30, wounding 50, and capturing 14 machine-guns; all achieved in a matter of minutes.

In the savage hand-to-hand fighting to clear the village the actions of newly commissioned Lieutenant G.M. (Morby) Ingram of the 24th Battalion stood out. Seizing an opportunity he led his platoon, which had been held down by German fire, in a charge that killed 40 and captured six machine-guns. Then, when again held down, he rushed several small posts. Once more forced to ground by German fire, he attracted the attention of a tank and, using it for cover, followed it with his platoon to the source of the fire. This was a quarry into which Ingram jumped, shooting several Germans, and forcing the surrender of 63 from a dug-out and capturing 40 machine-guns. Then, while his soldiers were mopping-up, he investigated a house from which a machine-gun had been firing and took a further 30 prisoners. His efforts earned him a Victoria Cross.

It is difficult to estimate the strength of the German defence, particularly considering the parlous state of their units. Most regiments were reduced to less than battalion strength yet, with remnants of at least two divisions holding the village, their numbers were probably far greater than that of the attackers. By 9 am, however, most of the village was in Australian hands, although they then had to withstand several counter-attacks. They then had to complete its clearance, in the course of which they found many more civilians.

It had been a successful and also costly attack. Bean describes Montbrehain as 'the last and one of the most brilliant actions of Australian infantry in the First World War'. They had taken 400 prisoners and a big haul of machine-guns. But it had cost them 30 officers and 400 men as casualties. Accepting Bean's estimation of the strength of each of the two infantry battalions at 240 then the battle had been catastrophic. The 21st Battalion, one of those slated for disbandment but granted a reprieve for this final action, lost 131 and the 24th Battalion 137: more than half their strengths, while the Pioneer Battalion lost 108. It was a heavy toll for the taking of one small French village on their last day of battle. The Hindenburg Line had cost the Australian Corps a total of 3,370 casualties.

***

Montbrehain once more displayed the discipline inherent in the AIF. Again they had gone into the cauldron and taken the terrible casualties. Bean even suggests they had gone into the battle 'light-hearted', cheered by rumours of German surrender and the thoughts of their forthcoming rest. These were definitely highly motivated men, and it was a motivation that reflected their discipline. On the one hand there was the collective military discipline to which they conceded, but probably of far greater importance was the self-discipline of the individual soldiers. Self-discipline is a rather nebulous term that we tend to associate with 'maturity' and 'experience' and link with motivation and self-control. It is a virtue not usually associated with young people, particularly males of the average age of the Diggers. Yet, in essence, it was their self-discipline that led these young men to 'jump the bags' again and again.

The self-discipline of the Digger was essential. It was needed on the long, exhausting marches: 'going up the line', marching hour after hour, the rhythmic thud of the boots on the dirt road, the slap of the bayonet scabbard on the thigh, the drag of the pack on the shoulders, and the dead weight of the rifle, and all the while thinking of what lay ahead. It took self-discipline to keep going to the next brief stop. It then took self-discipline to stand at the parapet in the cold and the rain and stare into the blackness, listening for the rattle in the wire and to fight the desperate urge to sleep. It took self-discipline to stomp behind the creeping barrage, or to leap up and charge the German machine-gun when the corporal yells 'Go'. The rules and regulations, the charge-sheets and jails, added motivation, but primarily it was his self-discipline that brought the Digger through. To describe him as a 'lovable larrikin' only shows an ignorance of his depth. Sadly it is a way still used by some to belittle him and his achievement.

CHAPTER 9

Conclusion

What these men did nothing can alter now. The good and the bad, the greatness and smallness of their story will stand. Whatever of glory it contains nothing now can lessen. It rises, as it will always rise, above the mists of ages, a monument to great hearted men; and, for their nation, a possession for ever.

C.E.W. Bean

On 5 October 1918 the Australian Corps, less its artillery and some specialist units, came out of the line and went into a long-needed rest by the banks of the Somme. Two days later they heard the news that the Germans were seeking negotiations, and then on 11 November, as they prepared to return to action, that the Armistice had been signed. Their war was over, yet for many it would be a further year before their arrival home.

The long wait for repatriation and demobilization was a frustrating time. In the British and Canadian armies it was a period of unrest and disorder yet the AIF weathered this testing-time without murmur. It reflected, under a different environment, the maturity of the Diggers and the soundness of their leadership and discipline. Once more it showed that the concern that they had reached a tipping-point of discipline in September had been exaggerated. While they had been very tired their morale had remained solid.

It is interesting to speculate on their feelings in the months that followed as they waited their turn for a ship home. They kept busy with more training, but this time with occupational courses to prepare them for 'civvy street'. After the euphoria of the war's end a sense of anti-climax must have descended. The teams were breaking up, the close mateships were ending. The security of living within the unit was over. No longer would they be fed, housed, moved and led but now had to face the prospect of looking after themselves, and making their own decisions. Most were young men, many of whom had come directly from school, and they faced the challenge of going into a new world; some would have considered it as daunting as the battlefield. Then back home they faced family, friends and new workmates who did not understand what they had been through and had their own perceptions of what the war had been like. The public was building its legends and would not want the truth to distort their imagining. Consequently the joy and relief of reunion would have been tinged with awkwardness.

Neither was there much in the way of a heroes welcome. The battalions returned in dribs and drabs with the individuals who had served longest coming home first and receiving their discharge. Hence there could be few welcoming parades or ceremonies. Nor was the public mood attuned to such celebration. Most families bore the scars from the war and there was a strong aura of public grief rather than of celebration. The reticence of the Digger began to settle in and he began to look forward to the comradeship of 'the one day of the year'. There, with those with whom he had shared the triumph and the horror he could find comradeship and understanding.

The Digger too was a different man than the one who had gone away. Even if not physically scarred, and over half of those who returned had been, there were the emotional wounds that were largely unrecognized by the public at the time. They had seen and done things that set them apart, and which were beyond the comprehension of family and friends. For most there would have been great difficulty in expressing their memories or of explaining their fears.

They would have found most Australians had failed to differentiate between 1918 and the preceding years of the war. The focus of the public imagining was fixed on the horror. It was the battles of 1916 and 17, the eighteen months from Fromelles to Passchendaele, that resonated in their thinking and it was from this period that most of their legends derived. The triumphs of 1918 did not fit comfortably with the public imagining and were therefore sidelined. The one period of which the Diggers were most proud was denied them.

***

With the start of the German Spring Offensive in March 1918 there had been a seismic shift in the character of the war. It was as if two boxers who for the opening rounds had fought in a clinch were now standing back and swinging wildly, first Germany, then as it tired the Allies, each looking for a knock-out blow. The nature of war had changed. Attack had supplanted defence as the dominant phase of war. Advances that had been measured in metres were now of kilometres. Infantry attacked dispersed, while it was now the artillery fire that was concentrated. Weaponry had been transformed: artillery shells had unprecedented accuracy and destructive power; the embryonic tank had mutated into a well-protected and reliable machine; there were now copious light-machine guns for the infantry; and there was a logistics system with trains and trucks to speed the shells and bullets to where they were needed. And there was a tactical concept, the combined-arms battle, to make use of these changes. The only thing that remained constant was the terrible 'body count'. The desperate thrashing by the protagonists ensured a 'butchers' bill' as great as in the previous years. And it was on this, rather than the triumph, that the public focused.

Just as the war had changed, so too had the Diggers. The hardened veteran of 1918 was very different from the 'new chum' who had fought so valiantly but hopelessly at Fromelles. The newly raised and loosely bonded battalions of 1916 were now tightly knit teams of very experienced fighting men who had created their own style of leadership and discipline. By 1918 they were well trained, skilled in battlecraft, and tactically competent. These factors led to confidence in themselves and to high morale, which bred the audacity with which they fought. They were among the very best soldiers on the Western Front. Yet this is not how we choose to remember them. It sits more comfortably in the public imagining for us to regard them as victims.

***

In early 1918 for the first time the Australians had faced the new 'shock' tactics of the German offensive. The Germans were suddenly able to shatter the tactical status-quo that had existed on the Western Front. Then when their offensive faded the BEF responded with its own new tactics and techniques. There was a new character to the war. It was more open and fluid, particularly as the Allied offensive gained momentum. For the previous eighteen months the Australians had fought the grinding battles of the Somme and Flanders. They had fought with courage and suffered terrible casualties but then in early 1918 they had seen their limited gains swept away by the German Spring Offensive. But the lives and the effort had not all been wasted. What they had learned in the hard years they translated into a battle-winning formula. The men had toughened and they had mastered the skills they needed for victory. And importantly their teams had bonded and they had confidence in themselves and their leaders. They had learned they were more than a match for the enemy. When all 5 Australian divisions came together in the new Australian Corps they constituted a very potent military force.

Their battles of 1918 reflected this skill and their newly established confidence. At Villers-Bretonneux and Hazebrouck they blocked the German offensive and their counter-attacks started the long haul to eventual victory. Their dominance over their enemy was proven in the phase of Peaceful Penetration. Then in four victorious battles of Hamel, Amiens, Mont St Quentin and the Hindenburg Line they made their major contribution to victory over Germany. In 1918, for the heavy cost of 10,500 lives and over 40,000 wounded, they advanced 60 kilometres, took 29,144 prisoners, captured 338 guns and liberated 116 towns and villages. It was a major achievement yet today it is seldom even acknowledged for the feat of arms that it was.

While war is not to be glorified, neither should the achievement of our soldiers be trivialized. We have allowed their victories to be obscured by the legends that have come to dominate the public imagining. The public has chosen, or been led, to ignore the triumph. Our art, architecture, literature, films, popular histories and memorial services all focus on the horror. For a hundred years the Australian public has viewed WW1 through a dark glass of legends. We have allowed our imagining of the war, and particularly its final year, to be distorted by those legends. It is time to put aside the legends and to seek a balance between the horror and the triumph.

***

Here seven of the most pervasive and influential legends have been considered against the operational performance of the Australian Corps in the final year of the war. Four of the seven legends are of Australian origin and three are foreign constructs we have embraced. Of the Australian four, two are positive – 'the lovable larrikin' and 'the born soldiers' – but neither is accurate and both obscure the truth. The other two Australian-related legends are in different ways particularly negative – 'a futile struggle' and 'warriors, not soldiers'. All the foreign legends – 'sheep to the slaughter', 'stabbed in the back' and 'lions led by donkeys' are negative. In essence the legends paint a bleak and negative picture of the Diggers' war and, in doing so, emphasise the horror.

In the introduction it was suggested we create legends to achieve four ends. It is instructive to measure the seven legends against those ends. Firstly that legends provide a simplified explanation of complex events. This is relevant to the legends 'sheep to the slaughter', which relates to morale, and 'lions led by donkeys', which concerns leadership. Both morale and leadership in their military context are complex issues and in applying simple shibboleths the public has trivialized the issues. The two legends were created with the intent of laying blame for the terrible casualties. Both fail to recognize the transformation of 1918 in the way the war was fought. The Digger did not see himself as a sheep nor his leaders as donkeys and in 1918 was proud of his contribution to victory.

Secondly that legends can mask unpleasant reality. To this end falls 'stabbed in the back'. The German General Staff sought to mask their failure by fabricating the *dolchstosslegende* which then, suiting the motives of several disparate groups, was widely promulgated. The claim that the German army was exhausted rather than defeated denies the reality of the superior tactics and strategy of the Allies. It was a fallacious but convenient argument for those who sought to deny the BEF, and with it the AIF, their victory.

Thirdly that legends are used to romanticize questionable behaviour. Here belong the two Australian legends, 'Aussies, the born soldiers', which is related to training, and the 'lovable larrikin', associated with discipline. The 'born soldier' was a flattering illusion; the Diggers success was in his training rather than his breeding. The legend of the 'lovable larrikin' was created to excuse the behaviour of a disruptive minority. It fails to take into consideration the various factors that impacted on discipline in the AIF, both negatively but predominantly positively. Nor does it recognise that by 1918 the AIF had forged its own style of discipline appropriate to a volunteer citizen army.

Finally that legends may be used to deliberately distort reality so that it can conform to a different agenda. This applies to a 'pointless struggle' which was championed by those opposed to the war for a variety of reasons. Although their opposition was political or ideological they sought to claim a moral high-ground from which to denigrate those who fought. Equivalently, the description by some senior British officers of the Diggers as 'warriors, but not soldiers', sniped at Australian discipline as a way to excusing the lesser battlefield performance of the average Tommy.

***

It would have been edifying to have asked the Digger, who was the subject of the legends, how he would have viewed them. Naturally he would have been curious as to how the legends depicted him: of who he was, what he did, and how he did it. The legends 'born soldier' and 'lovable larrikin' would have been quickly dismissed. While he would have enjoyed the flattery in the suggestion he was a born soldier he knew his success in 1918 was the product of his training and leadership. He saw the larrikin as disruptive and had been pleased few remained by 1918. He would have been amused to have been described as 'not really a soldier' by those British officers he often did not consider to be really warriors.

The legends 'lions led by donkeys' and 'sheep to the slaughter' he would have dismissed as inapplicable to the Australian Corps. He was a volunteer and was very proud of that status, and was certainly no sheep. Neither had his leaders been donkeys. His junior leaders had come from the ranks and led from the front. The senior Australian officers in 1918 had been skilled, innovative and humane.

'*Dolchtoss*' he would have considered as rubbish. He had played a significant part in the defeat of the German army and he knew it. He had fought Fritz in the hedgerows, and on the battlefields of Villers-Bretonneux, Hamel, Amiens, Mont St Quentin and the Hindenburg Line, and he had won each time. And often he had attacked and beaten equal and even greater numbers. His battlecraft and tactics had been superior and through his audacity he had shown he was more than a match for the German stormtrooper. Yes, he would say, the politics or ideology of some may lead them to claim the war had been a 'pointless struggle' but he had enlisted out of a sense of duty to Australia and the Empire for a cause in which he, and most of his countrymen believed. If he had the chance he would have concluded:

'Yes, it cost us dearly; nearly 60,000 lives, many of whom were my friends. But they died believing in their cause, and no way did they consider they had been tricked or duped. We fought and we suffered, and most of us continued to suffer in one way or another, for the rest of our lives. This was the personal horror we lived with, but that is only one half of our story.

'We achieved great things. We came from nothing; a rag-tag, untrained, ill-disciplined mob and in a short four years we welded ourselves into one of the finest armies the world has seen. Yet you have decided to forget our achievement and to emphasise the horror, or what you believe that horror was. You find it is less challenging to your contemporary society to ignore our triumph. It suits your focus on the victim. Yet we won great battles, and we won them on your behalf. Surely now is the time to give us credit and to recognize our triumph.'

***

Australians should have great pride in the achievement of the AIF in 1918. The Australian Corps' contribution to victory was out of proportion to its size. The eager mob of 1914 grew into a highly skilled army. In getting there they had developed their own style of leadership, discipline, battlecraft and training. In the face of terrible casualties they had built a force proud of its morale and esprit de corps. By 1918 it was an army with great unity, confidence and skill. The Diggers knew what they had achieved. They had borne the loss of friends and mates and had suffered the horror of the battlefield, but had fought their way to victory. As a nation we must always remember the lost and broken lives of those who stood on our behalf. Yet after a century it should become an issue of remembrance rather than one of grief or mourning. And with remembrance can come recognition of their accomplishment. For a hundred years we have allowed hollow legends to distort our understanding of that achievement. Now, at the centenary, we should at last celebrate their triumph.

Note on Strategy

While beyond the scope of this book, the following note is offered to help understanding.

The boundary between military and national strategy. Military strategy is a component of national strategy and is the art of the use of force, or the threat of force, to achieve the national objective. National strategy is the application of economic, political, psychological, technological as well as military means to secure the national objective. In WW1 the containment of the German Grand Fleet and the anti-submarine campaign were the principal contributions of the Royal Navy to British military strategy of the war. The blockade, denying Germany the resources to fight the war, was more an element of the national strategy. Earlier historians, including Basil Liddell Hart, contended it was the privations caused by the blockade that led to the collapse of political will, to *dolchstoss* and to capitulation. Later analysis has shown Germany had been 80% self-sufficient in food production in 1914. While there was a decline in food availability it was not to a critical level and what did occur is now largely attributed to mismanagement and the call-up of farm workers rather than to the blockade. The widely touted figure of 750,000 deaths from starvation is discredited, and with it credibility in the claim of the strategic impact of the blockade. Similarly, German industry was largely self-sufficient in natural resources with the exception of non-ferrous metals. The decline in its wartime production is now recognised as a product of organisational failure rather than the consequence of the blockade. While the blockade played its part it was not the decisive tool which it had been earlier regarded. Liddell Hart does however concede the psychological impact of the Hundred Days in weakening the will of the German civil and military leadership to prolong the war.

The boundary between tactics and military strategy. Until WW1 wars were usually fought in a single theatre for which a strategy was determined. WW1, the first *world-wide war,* was waged in many theatres (the AIF fought in six), each campaign with its own specific military strategy. This led to confusion as military strategy seemed to relate to geographically confined campaigns rather than to the overall conduct of the war. In an effort to resolve this confusion, over the last thirty years a new concept of an intermediate level of war between the strategic and tactical level has gained acceptance. This is termed the *Operational Level,* and applies to the conduct of campaigns within theatres of war. In this context the war on the Western Front is relegated to a campaign in a theatre and Foch's and Haig's strategies of 'the annihilation battle', or later of 'bite and hold', to those of operational concepts. Military strategy is thus restored to its proper status of defining how to achieve the military objectives as a component of the national strategy. This new concept of the Operational Level offers a sharper perspective of WW1 but I am yet to see a re-analysis of WW1 within these terms.

The Chain of Command in the Australian Corps and BEF in 1918

The numbers given here are well below the 'authorised establishment' strengths and reflect the erosion of manpower of 1918.

Section: 5 to 10 men commanded by a corporal

Platoon: 4 sections commanded by a lieutenant.

Company: 4 platoons, around 80–120 men, commanded by a captain.

Battalion: 4 companies, around 400–600 men, commanded by a lieutenant-colonel.

Brigade: 4 battalions, around 2000–3000 men, commanded by a brigadier-general.

Division: 3 brigades plus field artillery, commanded by a major-general.

Corps: 2 or 3 divisions (Australian Corps 5) plus medium artillery, commanded by a lieutenant-general.

Army: 2 or more corps commanded by a general.

Army Group: 2 or more armies (BEF in 1918 5) commanded by a field-marshal.

Notes

Chapter 1

1 *The Iliad of Homer*, translated by R. Lattimore, University of Chicago Press, Chicago, 1951, p. 125.
2 Dictionary definitions are from *The Macquarie Dictionary*, Macquarie Library Pty, Ltd, 1981.
3 G.F. Linderman, *Embattlers Courage:The Experience of Combat in the American Civil War*, The Free Press, New York, 1987, p. 1.
4 S.L.A. Marshall, *The Soldiers Load and the Mobility of a Nation*, The Combat Forces Press, Washington, 1950, p. 45.
5 Alan Seymour, *The One Day of the Year*, Angus and Robertson, Melbourne, 1958.
6 H. Mackay, *Turning Point, Australians Choosing Their Future*, Macmillan, Sydney, 1999.
7 L. Wilkins (ed.), *Artists in Action, from the collection of the Australian War Memorial*, Everbest Printing Co Ltd, Fishermans Bend, Vic.
8 Correli Barnett, 'The Western Front Experience as Interpreted through Literature', *RUSI Journal*, December 2003.
9 J. Winter, *Sites of Memory, Sites of Mourning, The Great War in European Cultural History*, Cambridge University Press, Cambridge, 1995.

Chapter 2

10 E. Blunden (ed.), *The Poems of Wilfred Owen*, Chatto and Windus, London, 1955, p. 80.
11 P. Simkins, *World War I The Western Front*, Colour Library Books Ltd, Surrey, UK, 1992, p. 154.
12 C.E.W. Bean, *Official History of Australia in the War of 1914–18, The AIF in France 1918*, Angus and Robinson, Sydney, 1937, Vol. V, Ch. IV and X.
13 Bean, *Official History of Australia in the War of 1914–18*, Vol. V, p. 18.

14 Ibid., Ch. X.
15 Ibid., p. 437.
16 Ibid., Ch. VIII.
17 Ibid., Ch. XI.
18 Barnett, 'The Western Front Experience'.
19 Bean, *Official History of Australia in the War of 1914–18*, Ch. XVI.

Chapter 3

20 *Mahabharata* retold by W. Buck, University of California Press, Berkeley, 1973, p. 265.
21 A useful insight to Irish-Australian attitudes is given in P. O'Farrell, *The Irish in Australia,* NSW University Press, Kensinfton, NSW, 1986, Ch. 6
22 The perspective of the radical Left is given in C.M.H. (Manning) Clark, *A History of Australia*, Volume VI, Melbourne University Press, 1987, Ch. 3, A Divided Australia, pp. 80–125.
23 The importance of legends is signalled in R. Ward, *The Australian Legend,* Oxford University Press, Melbourne, 1958.
24 T. Wilson, The peace settlement of 1919, in Ekins, A. (ed.), *1918: The Year of Victory*, Exisle, Auckland, 2010, p. 218.
25 Bean, *Official History of Australia in the War of 1914–18*, Vol. VI, p. 44.
26 Ibid., p. 42n.
27 Ibid., p. 34.
28 Ibid., Vol. V, p. 679.
29 Ibid., Vol. VI, pp. 57–60.
30 Ibid., pp. 54–5
31 Ibid., Ch. III.
32 Ibid., pp. 105–7.
33 Ibid., p. 376.
34 Ibid., pp. 650–3.
35 Ibid., pp. 403–7.
36 Ibid., p. 440.
37 Ibid., p. 440n.
38 P. Bobbitt, *The Shield of Achilles. War, Peace and the Course of History*, Penguin Books, London, 2003, pp. 24–64.

Chapter 4

39 Henry Reed, The Penguin Book of Contemporary Verse, K. Allott (ed.), Penguin Books, Middlesex, 1950, p. 236.

40 R. Coulthart, *Charles Bean*, Harper Collins, Sydney, 2014, pp. 89–90.

41 Ibid., pp. 15–22.

42 P. Rees, *Bearing Witness, The remarkable life of Charles Bean*, Allen and Unwin, Crows Nest, NSW, 2015, p. 129.

43 Coulthart, *Charles Bean*, pp. 55–63.

44 Ernest Scott, *The Official History of Australia in the War of 1914–18*, Vol. XI Australia During the War, Angus and Robertson Ltd, Sydney, 1936, p. 874.

45 Coulthart, *Charles Bean*, pp. 87–8

46 Ibid.

47 G. Wilson, *Bully Beef and Balderdash, Some Myths of the AIF Examined and Debunked*, Big Sky Publishing Pty Ltd, Newport, NSW, 2012, p. 110.

48 Coulthart, *Charles Bean*, pp. 91–2.

49 Wilson, *Bully Beef and Balderdash*, p. 114.

50 Bean, *Official History of Australia in the War of 1914–18*, Vol. VI, p. 22–4.

51 Detail for the Battle of Hamel is drawn from Bean, *Official History of Australia in the War of 1914–18*, Vol. VI, Ch. VIII and IX.

Chapter 5

52 C.J. Dennis, The Sentimental Bloke, Angus and Robertson, Sydney, 1950, p. 3.

53 Bean, *Official History of Australia in the War of 1914–18*, Vol. VI, pp. 1087–8.

54 Ibid., p. 1083.

55 Detail of the battle is drawn from ibid., Ch. VIII, IX, X, and G. Blaxland, *Amiens: 1918*, Frederick Muller, London, 1968.

56 S. Tetlow, Incorporating human factors in simulation: a British Army view, in M. Evans and A. Ryan, *The Human Face of Warfare, Killing, Fear and Chaos in Battle*, Allen and Unwin, St Leonards, NSW, 2000, p. 31.

57 D. Horner, *The Gunners. A History of Australian Artillery*, Allen & Unwin, St Leonards, NSW, pp. 173–82; R. Prior & T. Wilson, *Command on the Western Front, The Military Career of Sir Henry Rawlinson 1914–1918*, Pen & Sword Military Classics, Barnsley, UK, 1992.

58 W. Van der Kloot, 'Lawrence Braggs Role in the Development of Sound-

Ranging in World War 1', *Notes and Records of the Royal Society*, 59, pp. 273–84, 6 September 2005.

59 Bean, *Official History of Australia in the War of 1914–18*, Vol. VI, p. 936.

60 P.A. Pedersen, General Sir John Monash: Corp Commander on the Western Front, in D. M. Horner, (ed), *The Commanders. Australian military leadership in the twentieth century,* George Allen &Unwin, North Sydney, 1984, p. 98.

Chapter 6

61 *The Poems of Wilfred Owen*, p. 117.

62 E.J. Passant, *A Short History of Germany 1815–1945,* Cambridge University Press, 1969, p. 158

63 S. Badsey, Ninety years on: Recent and changing views on the military history of the First World War, in *1918 Year of Victory*, p. 258.

64 R. Prior, Stabbed in the Front: The German defeat in 1918, in *1918 Year of Victory*, pp. 52–3.

65 Bean, *Official History of Australia in the War of 1914–18*, Vol. VI, p. 1085. G. Serle, *John Monash: A Biography,* Melbourne University Press, Carlton, 1982, pp. 377–9.

66 B.H. Liddell Hart, *History of the First World War,* Cassell & Co Ltd, London, 1970, p. 460.

67 E. Warner, Douhet, Mitchell, Seversky: Theories of Air Warfare, in E. M. Earle (ed.), *Makers of Modern Strategy*, Princeton University Press, London, 1966.

68 B.H. Liddell Hart, *Strategy*, Faber & Faber Ltd, London, 1991, p. 201.

69 Badsey, Ninety years on, in *1918 Year of Victory*, pp. 247 and 252.

70 Blaxland, *Amiens*.

71 Serle, *John Monash*, p. 380.

72 Badsey, Ninety years on, in *1918 Year of Victory*, pp. 256–9.

73 Prior and Wilson, *Command on the Western Front*, pp. 77–80.

74 I.M. Brown, Feeding Victory: The Logistic Imperative Behind the Hundred Days, in P. Dennis and J. Grey (ed.), *1918 Defining Victory*, Army History Unit, Canberra, 1999, pp. 130–47.

75 N. Ferguson, *The Pity of War*, Penguin Press, Middlesex, 1998, pp. 248–67.

Chapter 7

76 The detail of the battle is drawn from Bean, *Official History of Australia in the War of 1914–18*, Vol. VI, Ch. XVIII, and with reference to M. Bomford, *Beaten Down by Blood, The Battle of Mont St Quentin-Peronne 1918*, Big Sky Publishing Pty Ltd, Newport, NSW, 2012.

77 *Manual of Land Warfare, 1. 6. 4. Staff Duties in the Field, Australian Army*, 1976, p. 3-1.

78 A. Clark, *The Donkeys*, Pimlico, UK, 2000.

79 Badsey, Ninety years on, in *1918 Year of Victory*, p. 245.

80 T. Cook, *1918 Year of Victory*, p. 181.

81 *Handbook on Leadership, 1973, Australian Army*, Defence Printing Establishment, Brunswick, Vic, pp. 3-1 to 3-3.

82 Bean, *Official History of Australia in the War of 1914–18*, Vol. VI, p. 1081n and J.M. Bourne, Conclusion, in *1918 Year of Victory*, pp. 40–1.

83 P. Stanley, *Men of Mont St Quentin Between Victory and Death*, Scribe Publications Pty Ltd, Carlton, Vic, 2009, gives a vivid account of the battle of 1 September from the perspective of a platoon of 21 Battalion.

84 *Handbook on Leadership*, p. IX.

85 Bean, *Official History of Australia in the War of 1914–18*, Vol. VI, p. 864.

86 Badsey, Ninety years on, in *1918 Year of Victory*, p. 248.

Chapter 8

87 S. Sassoon in *War Poetry*, J. Stallworthy (ed.), Oxford University Press, Oxford, 1988, p. 177.

88 Prior and Wilson, *Command on the Western Front*, pp. 346–8.

89 Details of the Battle for the Hindenburg Outpost Line are drawn from Bean, *Official History of Australia in the War of 1914–18*, Vol. VI, Ch. XIX, and Prior and Wilson, *Command on the Western Front*, pp. 346–57.

90 Ekins, *1918 Year of Victory*, p. 112.

91 Stanley, *Men of Mont St Quentin*, p. 118.

92 Ibid.

93 W. Moore, *The Thin Yellow Line*, Leo Cooper Limited, Hertfordshire, 1974, p. 153.

94 D. Grossman, Human factors in war: the psychology and physiology of close combat, in Evans and Ryan, *The Human Face of Warfare*, pp. 11–13.

95 Ibid., p. 7.

96 D. Grossman, *On Killing, the Psychological Cost of Learning to Kill in War and Society*, Little, Brown and Company, Boston, 1996, pp. 43–5.
97 *US Army Combat Stress Control Handbook*, Department of the Army, The Lyons Press, Connecticut, 2003, pp. 91–9.
98 Stanley, *Men of Mont St Quentin*, p. 91.
99 Moore, *The Thin Yellow Line*, p. 187.
100 The details of the mutinies is drawn from Bean, *Official History of Australia in the War of 1914–18*, Vol. VI, pp. 932–40, Ekins, *1918 Year of Victory*, pp. 116–21, and Stanley, *Men of Mont St Quentin*, pp. 209–11.
101 Detail of the Battle of the Hindenburg Line is drawn from Bean, *Official History of Australia in the War of 1914–18*, Vol. VI, Ch. XX and Prior and Wilson, *Command on the Western Front*, pp. 358–78.

Bibliography

Books

Bean, C.E.W., *The Australian Imperial Force in France, during the Main German Offensive, 1918. Vol. V, The Official History of Australia in the War of 1914–18,* 12 vols, Angus & Robinson, Sydney, 1937

Bean, C.E.W., *The Australian Imperial Force in France, during the Allied Offensive, 1918. Vol. VI. The Official History of Australia in the War of 1914–18,* 12 vols, Angus & Robertson, Sydney, 1942

Blaxland, G., *Amiens: 1918,* Frederick Muller, London, 1968

Bobbitt, P., *The Shield of Achilles. War, Peace and the Course of History,* Penguin Books, London, 2003

Bomford, M, *Beaten Down by Blood, The Battle of Mont St Quentin-Peronne 1918,* Big Sky Publishing Pty Ltd, NSW, 2012

Clark, A., *The Donkeys,* Pimlico, 2000

Clark, C.M.H. (Manning), *A History of Australia, Vol. VI,* Melbourne University Press, 1987

Coulthart, R., *Charles Bean,* Harper Collins, Sydney, 2012

Dennis, P., and Grey, J. (eds), 1918, *Defining Victory,* Army History Unit, Canberra, 1999

Earle, E.M. (ed.), *Makers of Modern Strategy,* Princeton University Press, London, 1966

Ekins, A. (ed.), *1918: The Year of Victory,* Exisle, Auckland, 2010

Evans, M., and Ryan, A. (eds.), *The Human Face of Warfare, Killing, Fear and Chaos in Battle,* Allen and Unwin, NSW, 2000

Ferguson, N., *The Pity of War*, Penguin Press, Middlesex, 1998

Grossman, D., *On Killing, the Psychological Cost of Learning to Kill in War and Society*, Little Brown and Company, Boston, 1996

Horner, D.M., *The Gunners: A History of Australian Artillery*, Allen & Unwin, NSW

Horner, D.M., *The Commanders: Australian Military Leadership in the Twentieth Century*, George Allen & Unwin, Sydney, 1984

Liddell Hart, B.H., *History of the First World War*, Cassell & Co Ltd, London, 1970

Liddell Hart, B.H., *Strategy*, Faber & Faber Ltd, London, 1991

Linderman, G.F., Embattlers *Courage: The Experience of Combat in the American Civil War*, The Free Press, New York, 1987

Marshall, S.L.A., *The Soldiers Load and the Mobility of a Nation*, The Combat Forces Press, Washington, 1950

Moore, W., *The Thin Yellow Line*, Leo Cooper Ltd, Hertfordshire, 1974

O'Farrell, P., *The Irish in Australia,* NSW University Press, Kensington, NSW, 1986

Passant, E.J., *A Short History of Germany 1815–1945*, Cambridge University Press, 1969

Prior, R., and Wilson, T., *Command on the Western Front. The Military Career of Sir Henry Rawlinson* 1914–18. Pen & Sword Military Classics, Barnsley, UK, 1992

Scott, E., *The Official History of Australia in the War of 1914–1918, Vol. XI Australia During the War*, Angus & Robertson Ltd, Sydney, 1936

Serle, G., *John Monash: A Biography*, Melbourne University Press, Carlton, 1982

Seymour, A., *One Day of the Year*, Angus & Robertson, Melbourne, 1958

Simkins, P., *World War I, The Western Front*, Colour Library Books, Surrey, UK, 1992

Stanley, P., *Bad Characters, Sex, Crime, Mutiny, Murder and the Australian Imperial Force,* Murdoch Books, NSW, 2000

Stanley, P., *Men of Mont St Quentin. Between victory and death*, Scribe Publications Pty, Ltd, Carlton, 2009

Ward, R., *The Australian Legend,* Oxford University Press, Melbourne, 1958

Wilkins, L. (ed.), *Artists in Action, from the collection of the Australian War Memorial*, Everbest Printing Co Ltd, Victoria

Wilson, G., *Bully Beef and Balderdash, Some Myths of the AIF Examined and Debunked*, Big Sky Publishing Pty Ltd, Newport, NSW, 2012

Winter, J., *Sites of Memory, Sites of Mourning, The Great War in European Cultural History*, Cambridge University Press, 1995

Pamphlets and Articles

Barnett, C., 'The Western Front Experience as Interpreted through Literature', *RUSI Journal*, December 2003

Van der Kloot, W., 'Lawrence Braggs Role in the Development of Sound-Ranging in World War I', *Notes and Records of the Royal Society*, (2005) 59, 273–84, 6 September 2005

Australian Army

Manual of Land Warfare, 1. 6. 4. Staff Duties in the Field, 1976

Handbook on Leadership, 1973

Land Warfare Doctrine 1: The Fundamentals of Land Warfare, 1998

US Army

Combat Stress Control Handbook, the Lyons Press, Connecticut, 2003

Index

Australian Army
AIF 7–13, 15–16, 22, 25–8, 30–1, 36–7, 39, 41, 50–1, 53, 63, 91, 104–3, 105–6, 108–9, 116–20, 122–5, 132–3, 135, 138, 142, 144, 146
Australian Corps
    1st Division 12, 21–2, 45–7, 98, 115–16, 127
    2nd Division 45, 56, 69–71, 74, 98–9, 103–4, 106, 110, 122, 127, 131, 133
    3rd Division 55, 69–71, 74, 98–9, 104, 127, 130
    4th Division 22, 55–6, 59, 71, 73–5, 115–16, 127, 131
    5th Division 71, 73, 75–6, 98, 106, 124, 127, 130–1
Australian Brigades
    5th Infantry Brigade 103–4
    6th Infantry Brigade 106, 133
    9th Infantry Brigade 22–3, 44
    12th Infantry Brigade 115
    13th Infantry Brigade 31–3
    14th Infantry Brigade 106
    15th Infantry Brigade 31–3, 107
Australian Battalions
    1st Battalion 45, 116, 127–8
    2nd Pioneer Battalion 133
    10th Battalion 46, 53
    14th Battalion 115
    17th Battalion 103
    18th Battalion 43
    19th Battalion 104, 106, 132
    20th Battalion 103
    21st Battalion 132–3, 135
    24th Battalion 133–5
    25th Battalion 132
    29th Battalion 132
    33rd Battalion 23
    36th Battalion 23, 28
    37th Battalion 132
    42nd Battalion 132
    46th Battalion 115
    47th Battalion 28
    48th Battalion 106, 115
    52nd Battalion 28
    53rd Battalion 110
    54th Battalion 132
    59th Battalion 129
    60th Battalion 132–3

British Army
British Fourth Army 21, 55, 64–6, 68, 70, 72, 74, 92, 98, 133
British Corps
    III Corps 45, 64, 66, 73, 115–16, 127, 129–30
    IX Corps 115–16, 129–30
British Divisions
    8th Division 30–31
    32nd Division 131
    46th Midlands Division 130–1
2/10th London Battalion 45

Canadian Army
Canadian Corps 64–5, 90

French Army
French First Army 64

German Army
German Divisions
    2nd Prussian Guards 103
    4th Guards 33
    228th Division 33

US Army
    US II Corps 133
    US 27th Division 130
    US 30th Division 130

***

Amess, Lt Albert 23
Amiens 9, 19, 21–22, 31, 44–5, 61–2, 64–6, 68, 70–4, 76–9, 81–2, 84, 86–7, 90–1, 93–5, 98–100, 115–16, 121, 126, 129, 132, 140, 143
Andrews, Sgt Harold 45
Anzac Cove 50, 53–4, 69, 78, 119
Arras 98, 113–14
Ashmead-Bartlett, Ellis 50
audacity 16, 42, 45–8, 140, 143
'Aussies, the born soldiers' 9, 49, 141–2
AWOL 118–19, 128

Bapaume 98, 114
battle procedure 99–100
battlecraft 9, 16, 26, 61–2, 69, 79, 87, 126, 140, 143–4
Bean, C.E.W. (Charles) 13–14, 23, 33, 40, 42–3, 45–6, 50–3, 62, 68, 110, 118, 122, 134–5, 137
Birdwood, General Sir William 21
Blackadder 86, 100
Blackburn, Lt Arthur 53–4
Blamey, Brig Gen Thomas 56
Blunden, Edmund 13, 29
Bridges, Maj Gen Sir William 51, 110

Bruggy, Sgt John 43–4
Bullecourt 16, 20, 55, 74

Caporetto 18
Chemin des Dames 18
Chipilly 45, 73, 127
Clark, Alan 100
Clemenceau, President Georges 59
collective triumph 4–6, 15, 24, 28–30, 84–5
combat stress 4, 123–4
Coxen, Brig Gen Walter 56
Currey, Pte William 110
Currie, Lt Gen Sir Arthur 92, 101, 129

Deist, Professor Wilhelm 84, 91
Dernancourt 22
desertion 119, 122, 124–8
discipline 9–10, 16, 24–6, 28, 63, 82, 95, 110, 116–22, 125–6, 128, 132–3, 135–6, 138, 140, 142–4
dolchstoss 83–5, 93, 142, 145
Douhet, Giulio 85

Elliott, Brig Gen Harold 'Pompey' 26, 31, 30–1, 42, 107, 110, 124, 129, 133
esprit de corps 24–5, 33, 126, 132, 144

'fighters, not soldiers' 9, 62
Flanders 2, 7, 15, 18, 21, 39–40, 65, 72, 86, 140
Foch, Marshal Ferdinand 21, 31, 64, 82, 91, 93–4, 146

Gallipoli 2, 7, 9, 12, 14–5, 23, 33, 37, 39, 46, 50, 53, 56, 62, 65, 69–70, 78, 100, 106, 110, 117–18, 122, 128
Gammage, Dr William 'Bill' 14
Gellibrand, Maj Gen John 47
German Spring Offensive 7–8, 18, 44, 59–60, 66, 87, 89, 93, 99, 139–40
Glasgow, Maj Gen William 26, 31–2, 43, 47
Gough, General Hubert 20
Graves, Robert 13, 29

Haig, Field Marshal Sir Douglas 18, 20, 22, 31, 33, 57, 62, 64, 76, 82, 85, 91–4, 98, 102, 120, 146
Hamel 9, 44, 49, 54, 58–9, 62, 66, 72, 82, 102, 110, 124, 140, 143
Harbonnieres 73
Hawke, Prime Minister Robert 'Bob' 12
Hayes, S/Sgt Jack 45, 127
Hazebrouck 21–2, 43, 46, 140
Heneker, Maj Gen William 31–2
Hindenburg Line 10, 33, 76, 83, 113–16, 127, 130–3, 135, 140, 143
Hines, Pte John 'Barney' 121
Hobbs, Maj Gen Talbot 47, 124
Hughes, Prime Minister William 'Billy' 36, 132–3
Hurley, Frank 13, 121

Ingram, Lt G.M 'Morby' 134
Irvine, Lt Arthur 44

Keating, Prime Minister Paul 12

leadership 9–10, 16, 24–6, 29, 31, 62–3, 82, 85, 97, 100, 102, 104–5, 107–10, 117–18, 126, 138, 140–1, 143–5
Leane, Brig Gen Raymond 106, 115
Learning Curve 91, 109
Leathley, Sgt Tom 46
legends 2–4, 6–12, 14–16, 20, 24, 82, 84, 86, 110, 138–9, 141–4
Liddell Hart, Capt Sir Basil 85, 145
Lihons 98
'lions led by donkeys' 9, 97, 100, 141, 143
Lloyd George, Prime Minister David 29, 85, 95
Lone Pine 42, 118
'lovable larrikin' 10, 113, 120, 136, 141–2
Ludendorff, Gen Eric 18, 21, 86, 114

Manning, Frederick 13, 29
Mannix, Cardinal Daniel 36
Marne 44, 60
McDougall, Sgt Stan 22
Monash, Lt Gen Sir John 13, 20, 47, 54–9, 69, 71, 79, 85, 90, 98–102, 106, 109, 123, 125–30, 133
Mont St Quentin 10, 33, 97–9, 101–4, 106–10, 140, 143
Montbrehain 133–5
morale 8, 12, 16–18, 22–7, 33–4, 39–41, 47, 62, 82, 85, 105, 108, 122, 126, 128, 133, 138, 140–1, 144
Morlancourt 44
Morshead, Lt Col Leslie 23
Murray, General Sir Archibald 54
mutiny 28, 109, 126–9, 132–3

Neck, the 42, 118

Oh What a Lovely War 86, 100
Operation *Georgette* 21, 23, 34, 40
Operation *Michael* 19–21, 23, 26, 30, 34, 40
Owen, Wilfred 13, 17, 29, 81

Passchendaele 16, 18, 20–1, 42, 72, 106, 110, 119, 139
Patterson, A.B. 'Banjo' 51
Peaceful Penetration 9, 35, 41–3, 46–8, 140
Peronne 98, 103–4, 106–7, 110, 129
Pershing, General John 56
personal horror 4–6, 8, 13–15, 24, 27–30, 143
Petain, Marshal Henri-Philippe 21
Plumer, General Sir Herbert 47
'pointless struggle' 2, 8–9, 35–7, 48, 142–3
Pozieres 20, 42, 54, 110
Pryor, Professor Robin 14
Post-Traumatic Stress Disorder (PTSD) 4, 40, 124
public horror 6, 30
public imagining 3, 9–10, 13–16, 50–1, 139–41

Quinn's Post 118

Rawlinson, General Sir Henry 21, 31,

33, 64, 92–3, 98, 102–3, 115–16, 129, 133
Robertson, General Sir William 85
Rosenthal, Maj Gen Charles 22–3, 26, 43–5, 47, 110

Sassoon, Siegfried 13, 29, 113
Schlieffen, General Count von Alfred 88
Schwarz, Lt Walter 126
'sheep to the slaughter' 8, 17–18, 28, 141, 143
Shell Crisis 95
Sinclair-Maclagan, Maj Gen Ewen 47, 56, 58
Somme 2, 7, 15, 20, 24, 30, 40, 45, 64, 70, 73, 77, 86, 97–9, 103, 106, 138, 140
'stabbed in the back' 9, 81, 84, 141–2
Stacy, Lt Col B.V. 'Bertie' 128
strategy 54, 65, 81–2, 87, 91–5, 109, 142, 145–6
Suez 12, 86

tactics 6, 8, 11, 16, 19, 26, 43, 60, 62, 78, 81–2, 87, 89–92, 95, 106, 109, 126, 140, 142–3, 146
Treasure, Lt Cecil 40

Villers-Bretonneux 22–3, 26, 28, 30–3, 44, 140, 143

Watson, Maj Stan 78–9
Wazza, the 118, 120
Wilder-Neligan, Lt Col Maurice 46, 106
Wilkins, Hubert 13, 68
Wilson, President Woodrow 83
Wilson, Professor Trevor 14

About the Author

Pat Beale served as an officer in the Regular Army for thirty years during which he saw active service in the later days of the Malayan Emergency; the Confrontation in Borneo, where he was awarded the Military Cross; and then in Vietnam, where, as a member of the Australian Army Training Team, he was attached to the US Special Force. There he commanded a battalion of hills' tribesmen which he led in the intense ten-day battle of Dak Seang, for which he was awarded a Distinguished Service Order for gallantry and a US Silver Star while his battalion received the prestigious US Valourous Unit Citation.

He had a varied career: he was at Maralinga in the days of the last nuclear tests; served with the Pacific Islands Regiment at Wewak in PNG; with the Malaysian Army as a tactics instructor; and as the commander of 1st Battalion, the Royal Australia Regiment. He is a graduate of ANU, and the Army and Defence Staff Colleges where, at the latter, he also served on the staff as director of strategic studies. He is well qualified to write on issues of combat stress, fear and courage and, from the experience of his career, on leadership, training, discipline, tactics and strategy. In his final years in the Army he held senior intelligence and security appointments. He is now retired and living in the Adelaide Hills.

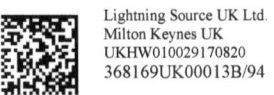

Lightning Source UK Ltd.
Milton Keynes UK
UKHW010029170820
368169UK00013B/94